Creative

Intarsia

Projects

Garnet Hall

Sterling Publishing Co., Inc. New York

A Sterling/Tamos Book

A Sterling/Tamos Book
© 2003 Garnet Hall

Note   Patterns may be copied for the purpose of making projects

Sterling Publishing Co., Inc.
387 Park Avenue South
New York, NY 10016-8810

TAMOS Books Inc.
300 Wales Avenue
Winnipeg, MB Canada R2M 2S9

10 9 8 7 6 5 4 3 2 1

Distributed in Canada by Sterling Publishing Co., Inc.
c/o Canadian Manda Group, One Atlantic Avenue, Suite 105
Toronto, Ontario, Canada M6K 3E7
Distributed in Great Britain and Europe by Cassell PLC,
Wellington House, 125 Strand, London WC2R 0BB, England
Distributed in Australia by Capricorn Link (Australia) Pty Ltd.
P.O. Box 704, Windsor, NSW 2756 Australia

Photography Jerry Grajewski, grajewski•fotograph.inc,
        Winnipeg Canada

Printed in Hong Kong

National Library of Canada Cataloguing in Publication Data

Hall, Garnet, 1949-
        Creative intarsia projects / Garnet Hall.

        Includes index.
        "A Sterling/Tamos book".
        ISBN 1-895569-86-9

1. Marquetry--Technique. I. Title.
TT192.H342 2002   745.51'2   C2002-911062-9

        Library of Congress Cataloging-in-Publication Data

Hall, Garnet, 1949-
    Creative intarsia projects / Garnet Hall.
        p. cm.
    "A Sterling/Tamos book."
    ISBN 1-895569-86-9
      1. Marquetry. I. Title.

    TT192 .H37 2003
    745.51'2--dc21   2002042877

Tamos books Inc. acknowledges the financial support of the Government of Canada through
the Book Publishing Development Program (BPIDP) for our publishing activities.

Note   If you prefer to work in metric measurements, to convert inches to millimeters multiply
by 25.4.

The advice and directions given in this book have been carefully checked, prior to printing, by
the Author as well as the Publisher. Nevertheless, no guarantee can be given as to the project
outcome due to the possible differences in materials and construction and the Author and
Publisher will not be responsible for the results.

ISBN 1-895569-86-9

Contents

Introduction   3
Tools for Intarsia   5
        Cutting Tools   5
        Shaping and Sanding Tools   7
        Special Effects Tools   9
                carving   9
                wood burning   9
                sandblasting   9
                wire brushing   10
                burnishing   10
                stamping on damp wood   10

Transferring Patterns   10
Fitting   11
Raising and Lowering   13
Backing and Glue-up   15
Finishing   16
Workshop Safety   16
Wood Colors   20
Being Creative   24

Projects

Moonflight   27
Rearing Horse   34
Thunderbird   38
Nativity Scene   43
Wizard and Dragon   53
German Shepherd   57
Fish Through a Porthole   61
Parrot   65
Raccoon in a Tree   69
Eagle's Catch   73
Prairie Lilies   77
Mirror Art   80
Ducks in the Reeds   83
Owl Bank   91

Index   96

*I*ntarsia, the popular craft of wood inlay, is for me the most creative art form there is. Choosing beautiful pieces of wood, cutting them, and fitting the different textured and colored pieces into a design that I have visualized is greatly satisfying and an achievement providing much pleasure. The creative opportunities are endless. Every new piece of wood provides an idea and the combination of colors and wood grain patterns can produce spectacular designs.

The term intarsia comes from the Latin verb *interserere*, meaning to insert. The inlaying of wood pieces was the technique of the old masters, which provided the magnificent patterns and shapes that decorated panels in churches and buildings. Their work often rivaled painting in the ability to convey expression and perspective. Instead of paint, however, the intarsia artists used different shades of wood and the subtle arrangement of wood grains to create their effects. They accomplished their woodworking magic with only the simplest of tools, usually a pocket knife and a gouge.

Modern intarsia artists have proceeded in new ways. Many modern tools and techniques make their work appear quite different from the old masters. The colors and textures of wood and the arrangements of these to form pictures are still an important aspect of today's designs. However, perspective is gained by raising, lowering, and shaping the different wood pieces. The depth achieved by modern artists approaches relief carving. Indeed, the cut out pieces of wood are raised and lowered according to a prearranged plan and the finished work is dimensional.

I have been involved with intarsia for many years and the creative possibilities always present new challenges. Whether you use a pattern or create your own design there are many considerations that demand your full attention. Which woods to use, how to shape the pieces, how much perspective to give the work, and which finish is suitable must all be carefully thought out. Over the years I have developed many new techniques that I will pass on to you in this book. I will also share ideas and methods discovered while conducting classes and seminars at woodworking shows. My intarsia art today is the product of the knowledge I have gained and will evolve as I continue to learn..

In this book I hope to expand the creative aspects of intarsia. I include fourteen fairly complex projects with how-to details on every aspect

This project resembles free standing sculpture and utilizes natural material, stained glass, painted and unpainted wood, as well as regular intarsia

A wood-burning tool is used to burn in the stamens and spots on the petals for these intarsia lilies

of their construction. I also include new techniques that I have discovered and other skills that I have adapted to make them more useful to intarsia art. I include sandblasting techniques to add texture to wood so that it will look weathered or like driftwood as well as instructions on how to turn western red cedar a dark shade, how to add shading and depth by wood burning, how to add interest by burnishing, how to do scrolling and wire brush techniques, and how to create a sandblasting effect by using a torch and wire brush. You will also see how enhanced 3-D can add perspective to bring a project to life. The use of stains is also discussed. Another idea is nondirectional intarsia that is cut from one board so grain direction is not an issue and fitting is easy. These pieces are usually painted. Intarsia projects can also be made free standing to look like sculpture. These techniques will add interest to any intarsia project.

If you are a beginner to intarsia, you will find it helpful to read my first book, *The Art of Intarsia*, which describes basic steps and outlines simple to intermediate projects. Once the beginning skills are mastered you will have no trouble with the projects in this book. How-to photographs and step-by-step explanations are provided for all techniques. Wood selection guides are included as well as tools needed for each project and ways to adapt tools that you have already at hand. Some of the projects are more difficult than others, but each offers the opportunity for your special input. Intarsia is creative and rewarding, and most of all it's fun to do.

This project combines staining, natural wood, and texturing and the wood can be distressed with a wire brush, small propane torch, or a sandblaster

Although intarsia looks like a complex art form the artist does not need a workshop stocked with an array of expensive tools to make exquisite pieces. Basically the requirements are tools to cut and sand. I will list the essential tools and the alternatives that I have found work well for the job. Many of the tools you have in your workshop can be adapted for intarsia work, as I will show in the following pages.

Cutting Tools

BASIC SAWS

The saws most often used for cutting out the pieces are the scroll saw and the band saw. Each has advantages and disadvantages. Although I now prefer a scroll saw for intarsia work, for years I used a band saw with very satisfying results. In a perfect world, having both saws is the best solution.

SCROLL SAW

If you can have only one cutting tool, a scroll saw is the most useful for intarsia work. The cutting rate has improved with the new types of blades. The fastest blade used to cut the ¾ in material that is most popular for intarsia work is the precision ground style. However, it cuts very aggressively making it more difficult to follow a cutting line , especially if you are new to scrolling. A double tooth reverse blade cuts more slowly and allows more time to make the corners. I prefer a #7 precision ground style blade or a #7 double tooth reverse blade for cutting ¾ in softwoods such as western red cedar and pine. For harder woods I use a #9 precision ground style or double tooth reverse blade and for thinner woods and backing boards I use a #5 precision ground style or double tooth reverse blade. I also like a full reverse style blade which also leaves a smooth edge and a splinter-free bottom cut. A reverse blade will clean up the fuzzies on the bottom of the pieces, but a disadvantage is that this blade will cause the wood to hop more.

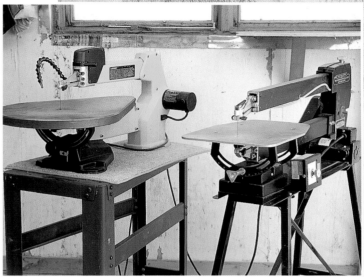

Typical scroll saws (above) and band saw (below)

Generally, scroll saws leave smooth edges so less sanding is required. A 16 in throat is adequate, but a larger saw is more useful. For more versatility choose an 18 in or 20 in saw. A 30 in Excalibur is the largest saw available and should meet any scrolling need. Scroll saws make tight corners and do inside cuts with ease. Use a blade lubricant to extend the blade life. It also makes cutting hardwoods and thicker woods easier.

BAND SAW

If you have only a band saw in your workshop and you want to do intarsia work you don't have to run out and buy a scroll saw immediately. Here are a few tips that I have found useful to make the band saw work as well as the scroll saw for your intarsia needs. The band saw won't do inside cuts as well as a scroll saw but the following technique will work.

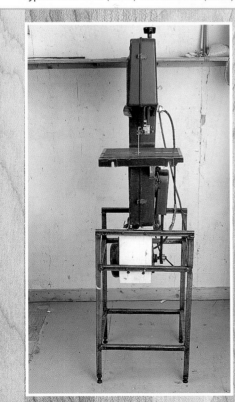

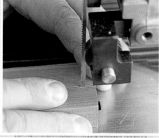
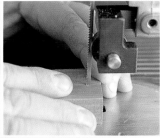

1 Cut into the inside cut following the grain of the wood.
2 Make the inside cut.
3 Shut off the saw and back the blade out along the cut.
4 Squeeze some glue into the cut.
5 Clamp it shut.
6 When the glue has dried, sanding the cut will completely disguise it.

The blades used on a band saw won't cut as tight a radius as a scroll saw but this can be improved. I use a ⅛ in blade 14-15 TPI. A ¹⁄₁₆ in blade is harder to track but is helped with the Carter stabilizer which has a groove for the blade to run in. Rounding the back of the blade also helps. The use of cool (guide) blocks which can be run tight to the blade reduce twisting of the blade and enable you to make tighter turns. These can be purchased or you can make your own from a hardwood such as teak or lignite vitae. Blade lubricants also help the blades to make tight turns by reducing friction. Make sure the blade has proper tension. If the blade is too loose it will wander off the line and will not make good turns.

I run my blades tighter than recommended on the saw's gauge. They track and turn better, although this may shorten the life of the blades. Judge the tension by sound or movement of the blade. The sound should be a C or G note. Tighten the blade by the gauge and then grasp the blade between thumb and index finger half way between the guide assemblies. The blade should move ⅛ to ³⁄₁₆ in with reasonable pressure. Then give it another half turn on the tensioning knob. Pluck the blade and try to memorize the pitch.

Read left to right, each row **1** Cutting in with the band saw **2** Making the inside cut **3** Backing out of the cut with saw off **4** Squeeze glue into the cut **5** Clamp until glue dries **6** Sand smooth and the cut line disappears

Read left to right, across
1 Guide blocks help make tighter turns
2 The Carter stabilizer helps keep the blade on track
3 Lubricating the blade helps to make tighter turns
4 Rounding the back of the blade for better tracking

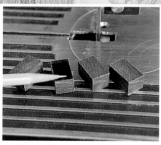
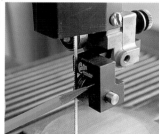

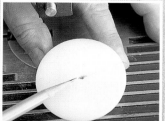

Read left to right
1 Zero clearance inserts keep small pieces from falling into the body of the saw
2 Fuzzies need to be sanded off for proper fit

Zero clearance plastic inserts are useful for cutting small pieces. You cut in the blade slot which will be the width of the blade. The plate will support the small pieces and they won't fall into the body of the saw. The plastic inserts won't damage the blades even if you push the blade into the insert. But if you are hitting the insert you are probably pushing the wood into the blade too hard or the blade may be dull causing you to push harder. Band saws cut faster than scroll saws do, which may be important for production work, but because they cut only downward they leave splinters or fuzzies as they exit the wood and these require sanding. Sand only the edges on the outside of the project. Inside edges won't be seen.

Band saws leave wider kerfs than scroll saws do, which will leave slightly wider gaps between pieces. However, band saws are useful for resawing pieces thinner for lowering. Both scroll saws and band saw have distinct advantages and it would be good to have both saws in your workshop.

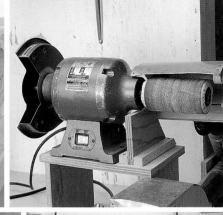

Shaping and Sanding Tools

Once the pieces are cut out they are ready for shaping. You can adapt almost any abrasive tool to this process. A belt sander or larger pneumatic sander with an 80-grit belt is the best way to remove excess material quickly. If you want one tool to do a multiple of jobs, choose a small pneumatic sander in a flex shaft or power carver. Begin with an 80-grit sleeve, inflated firm, to remove excess material quickly. Then use a 120-grit sleeve with less inflation to do more refined sanding and finish the sanding with a 220-grit sleeve.

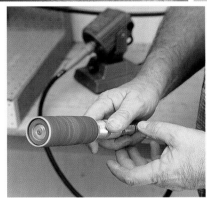
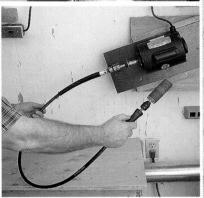

> *Note* Sandstorm sanders should not be used over 5000 RPM. Foredom's high torque, low RPM carver called Series L, works very well with small pneumatic sanders. It is variable speed with a maximum RPM of 5000. The high torque feature allows it to remove material quickly at low RPM without powering out. There are other power carvers that you can use. Try to find the tools that work best for you.

Another alternative is a Flex shaft. The best type has bearings in both ends. Wolfcraft has a heavy-duty model with a maximum RPM of 6000, which is more than adequate. It can be chucked into a drill press or hooked directly to an electric motor. The fastest motor that is readily available is a 3450 RPM, but a 1725-RPM motor will also work very well. This motor is slower, but is easier to find. There are a number of adapters on the market to attach the shafts to motors.

Read left to right, each row **1** 6-in stationary belt sander **2** Large pneumatic sander **3** Sandstorm sander chucked into a power carver **4** Sandstorm sander chucked into a flex shaft **5** Flex shaft chucked into a drill press **6** Hard rubber drum in a drill press **7** An adapter used to attach shafts to a motor to adapt other sanders

Note I am constantly asked about using a router with a rounding overbit to do the shaping for intarsia work. I don't recommend it. Routers are great tools for the jobs for which they are intended, but using them for routing small pieces of wood can be a dangerous practice. Woods such as cedar tend to splinter easily, which can damage the wood piece. Also router use leaves the work looking uniform and machine-made. The handmade look is lost.

You can adapt a number of other tools for sanding such as portable belt sanders, palm sanders, as well as 4-in and even 1-in belt sanders. Sanding can even be done with wood rasps and files. In fact a drum sander in a drill press, hand drill, or chucked onto a motor will work. Small hand-held Dremel type tools are used by many people. Basically any tool that will remove wood should work for the shaping step—even 80-grit sandpaper if you have the arm energy. Intarsia is often called sandpaper carving.

The fine sanding step doesn't offer as many solutions. Other than fine sandpaper I have found only a few tools that will speed up this process. I have had good results with a Merit flap sander or a star twister for the finest sanding. The twister uses alternating layers of star-shaped sandpaper that twists to form a flexible sanding surface for sanding irregular surfaces. With coarse grit paper it will also texture wood.

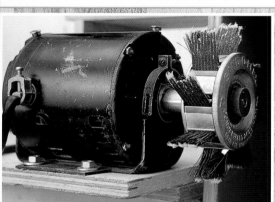

Left A flap sander *Right* A star twister are used for the fine sanding

The irregular shape of some intarsia pieces causes many shaping and sanding problems. I have found a number of tools that help in these cases.

Left Small hard rubber drum *Center* Cone sander *Right* Rasps and grinders

1 A small hard rubber drum can get into spaces down to about ½ in.
2 Cone shaped spiral sanders will get down to about ¼ in.
3 A selection of rotary rasps and grinders is a good investment. These can be used in a Foredom power carver or a flex shaft. Also, small hand-held Dremel tools have a selection of small rasps and grinders in their kit.
4 A detail sander by Rencrafts is a versatile hand tool that will access many tight spaces. It works for shaping as well as sanding.
5 A series of hard drums by Foredom is very aggressive and excellent for shaping hardwoods. The drums remove material quickly but they must be used carefully. If they slip off the wood and hit your hand, you will be injured, so wearing a leather glove is advisable. In spite of the danger, however, I wouldn't be without them for shaping hardwoods.
6 There are a number of differently shaped flap wheels available. They differ from the Merit and twister wheels because the sandpaper is not replaceable. They can be helpful in certain situations.

Read left to right
1 Rencrafts detail sander shapes and sands
2 Hard drums for shaping hardwood

7 Sandpaper wrapped around various size pieces of wood will get into unusual places. Small emery boards used to file fingernails can also be useful to sand small places. They can be easily formed into different shapes or cut the shape you need from plywood and glue on the grit of sandpaper you want.

There may be other sanding tools that could be used. If you discover something that works for you it should be included in your tool arsenal. Don't overlook anything that can be used or adapted. It isn't necessary to buy all these tools at once. Add them when you can. Each one will make your work quicker and easier.

Read left to right **1** Selection of flap wheels **2** Sandpaper wrapped dowels **3** Make your own sandpaper shapes

It is possible to extend the range and scope of intarsia by incorporating appropriate special effects into the projects. This can be done by using different tools to create textures and effects for a unique appearance. A great many different effects are possible with these tools. The only limit is your own imagination. The following is a list of various tools that can be used to achieve unusual ways to enhance intarsia projects. Specific uses for these techniques and descriptions of their use will be given as they are applied to the actual projects in the book.

Special Effects Tools

CARVING A number of power rasps that are made to be used in power carvers will enable you to add carving details into intarsia pieces as well as shape them in difficult situations. There are power carvers available that operate on air at very high RPMs allowing for very fine detail work in almost any material including glass.

WOOD BURNING A good quality wood burner allows the addition of various details to projects. The art of burning images onto different materials is called pyrography. This tool is capable of many things and if you plan to utilize extensive wood burning in your projects you can learn more about the art from the many books available on the subject. I use wood burning details mainly for claws and eyes. It's also useful to add detail to trees, such as the black bark marks on birch trees. Shading is another area where wood burning is helpful.

SANDBLASTING A sandblaster is useful for texturing wood and achieving interesting effects. A blasting cabinet is the safest way to do blasting and it will allow you to recover some of the sand. Be sure to wear face protection when sandblasting without a cabinet.

Above **1** A wood burning tool is used to add details *Right* **2** Small sandblasting cabinet

With a small sandblaster a good face shield is adequate. Larger units require a hood. Having a cabinet is the best and safest way to proceed. It may be purchased or you can build your own.

WIRE BRUSHING A wheel style wire brush can be used in a hand drill, flex shaft, or as a stationary piece to give wood the appearance of hair on an animal's coat. It helps to dampen the wood first. Be sure to use eye protection when using a wire wheel. A full-face shield is best.

BURNISHING A fiber style wheel can be used to burn the wood creating a shading effect.

STAMPING At one time I did leather work and I kept all the leather stamps. Now I use them to make interesting designs in wood. The stamps leave their imprints in damp softwood, such as western red cedar or pine. I have used leaf pattern stamps with good results. I intend to try others as ideas materialize.

Transferring Patterns

The patterns in this book need to be enlarged to make them actual size. Permission is given to copy them for your own use only. You can also order the patterns (see p 96).

Enlarging

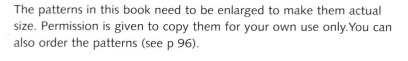

You can photocopy the pattern, enlarging it to the required size and taping all the sheets together (please allow for a margin of error of 1 or 2 percent). Or you can have the pattern copied by a blueprint company. They will produce an accurate, exact copy.

Putting Patterns on Wood

Once the pattern is the correct size there are three ways to transfer it onto the wood.

1 TRACE the pattern pieces onto the wood with carbon paper. Place the pattern on the wood grain you have chosen and slip the carbon paper under it. Trace around the pattern lines firmly with a sharp pencil or ballpoint pen. Be accurate.

2 PHOTOCOPY the patterns, cut out the various paper pieces, and glue them onto the wood. Gluing the pieces can be messy so be sure you clean the residual glue off the wood.

Spray glue, glue sticks, or rubber cement all work. Paint thinner works best for taking the paper off and cleaning up the glue. It evaporates quickly and then the wood can be sanded.

A new variation of the photocopy method is to make photocopies of the project and transfer them to the wood with a new tool called The Transfer Tool. This simple tool melts the plastic toner onto the wood. One small problem is that you have to turn the paper over, so the toner side is down, thus you are tracing the pattern onto the wood in reverse. To overcome this problem, once you have the pieces cut out, turn them over so that the project is as it was originally on the pattern. There is a special paper on which to photocopy the pattern. This produces a sharper image and is easier to transfer.

3 MAKE A TEMPLATE of the project out of a thin material such as ⅛ in baltic birch plywood or hardboard. Place the pattern onto the wood and slip the carbon paper under it. Tape down with masking tape. Trace. You can also spray glue the entire pattern onto the template material. Cut out the pieces and leave the pattern on the template pieces. Cut out the pattern on the line with a scroll saw (use #3 or #5 double or regular tooth blades with saw running at 1000 SPM strokes per minute). When template is cut out, mark on it all grain direction instructions, shade suggestions, thickness of wood, etc. This is helpful when cutting more pieces. Clean up the edges with sandpaper. The template is now ready to trace on wood. Store templates in a pizza box. This method requires the extra step of making the template, but once made it can be used over again. This saves much time. I prefer this method because it gives me the best fit.

Above **1** Use a transfer tool to transfer pattern onto wood
Below **2** Make a template from plywood

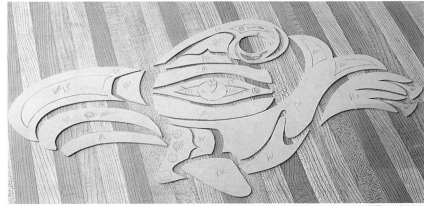

Right Be sure to outline with the pencil held at an angle. If held straight up the pieces will be larger and cause fitting problems.

Fitting

Fitting can be the most frustrating part of the intarsia project. Cutting the pieces carefully is the most important first step. Accurate cutting is necessary, and the ability to do this comes with practice. I cut right on the line with the narrowest blade that will cut the wood efficiently. Make sure the blade is square to the table so that the cuts are even and not sloping. If the pieces are cut exactly to the pattern, fitting them together is not difficult.

To test for saw square to table cut a shallow kerf in a piece of wood, shut the saw off. Turn the piece of wood around so the kerf mark is facing the back of the saw blade. If the back of the blade fits into the kerf the blade is square to the table.

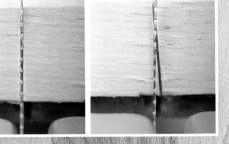

Above left **1** Trim for fit by running a saw blade between the pieces
Right **2** Carbon paper marks high spots between pieces

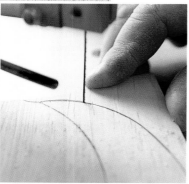

Above Left **1** To make inside piece trace the opening onto the correct wood *Right* **2** When cutting the piece cut outside the line

Method 1

Cut out all the pieces and begin to fit them. Sometimes the pieces will fit right off the saw. This is a magic moment and doesn't happen often.

I begin in the middle of free-form pieces or in the corners if the piece is framed. When pieces don't go together exactly, hold them tightly together and run a saw blade between them. Then look between the pieces, mark the high points, and sand or saw these down. A lightbox can be used effectively to mark these high points.

Another way to mark the high points is to place a strip of carbon paper between the pieces, push the pieces together, and the high points will leave a black mark on the wood, which can then be removed.

Sometimes the trimming and sanding don't work, and you have no choice but to remake a piece. Templates are very useful at these times. When the project has inside pieces to fit, it is easier to use the opening to draw an outline for the inside piece. When cutting out this piece cut outside the line leaving the line showing. If you cut carefully the piece should fit or be very close so that you can insert the piece into the opening. Then find a space to insert the scroll saw blade and cut the piece into place by cutting down the line where the pieces meet. You can also fit the opposite way. Cut out the inside piece first, then trace it onto the shade of wood you are using for the larger piece. Cut inside the line.

Method 2

This building method fits the project one piece at a time and works best on smaller projects, under 40 pieces. Begin with one of the larger pieces, cut it out, and use it to mark the common line between it and a piece it touches, shown at left. Cut the touching piece out and use both pieces held together to mark the common line between the next piece that the two pieces touch. Work your way through the project one piece at a time (see pictures at left). This method is slower than the first but is more forgiving if your cutting skills are just developing. However, mistakes in cutting can become amplified from one piece to the next until the entire project becomes distorted, so this method works best for smaller projects with fewer pieces.

Method 3

This sand-to-the-line method is the slowest of all the methods, but it can give good results if you don't have much experience following a line with a scroll saw. Cut outside the line and sand the pieces to the line with a spindle sander. An oscillating spindle sander works well. A drum sander mounted in a drill press will also work. It is helpful to mount a wood table on the metal one. Drill a hole in this table so the drum sits down in the hole, as shown, below right.

Side pressure on the drum will damage the drill spindle over time. Lee Valley makes a nice jig with a live center that attaches to a drill press table and supports the bottom of the sanding drum. A few different sizes can be helpful. The bigger drums remove material faster but you will need the small ones for tight corners. Some inside cuts won't be able to be sanded, so they will have to be cut on the line.

There may be other methods of fitting and you will evolve what works best for you. I use any one of the three methods (plus the curse-and-pitch method) in different situations.

Finally, if your project doesn't fit airtight don't be upset. If I am within a saw kerf or $1/16$ in I am satisfied. Fitting becomes more accurate with practice. Take your time, cut carefully, and you will be amazed how quickly you will improve.

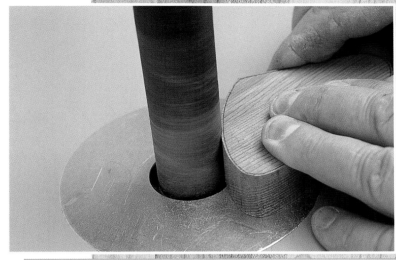

Above Sanding to the line *Below* Drill hole in wood table so drum sits down in the hole

Raising and Lowering

Raising and Lowering Guide

R Raise $1/8$ in	L Lower $1/8$ in
R1 Raise $1/4$ in	L1 Lower $1/4$ in
R2 Raise $3/8$ in	L2 Lower $3/8$ in
R3 Raise $1/2$ in	L3 Lower $1/2$ in

The patterns in this book are raised and lowered in increments of ⅛ in. To raise a base material that is ¾ in thick, glue scrap plywood cut to size of piece to the bottom of the piece. Clamp until dry. Reserve any scrap ⅛ in and ¼ in plywood, usually from backing material, for this purpose. This works well for interior pieces to be raised.

If the piece to be raised is on the outside of a project use the same type and shade of wood as the piece itself, because the raised piece (plywood) will show. To save time I sort out all the pieces to be raised ⅛ in and glue them onto one large ⅛ in board. Then I do the same with all the pieces to be raised ¼ in and any other increments. When the glue is dry I set my saw at an angle and cut out the pieces.

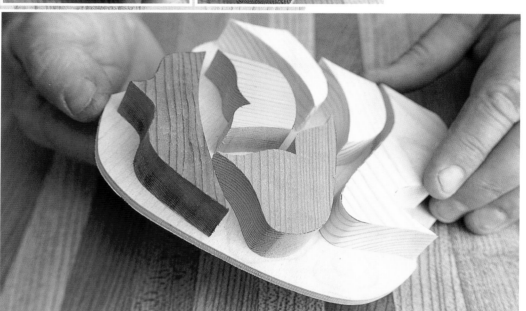

To lower a piece, resaw it thinner. Scroll saws are limited to 1½ in thick wood. Anything thicker should be resawn on a band saw or sand the pieces thinner. To lower a base material ¾ in thick measure and mark final amount to be removed with a pencil line that can be followed with the saw.

Top Left **1** To raise, glue scrap plywood to bottom Top Right **2** Raise outside piece with the same wood as project piece Center **3** Glue all pieces to be raised the same amount to a common board Above **4** Draw reference lines to guide shaping. Do not shape below reference line

If you use MDF to make a project, this material comes in various thicknesses and you can purchase what you need thus eliminating raising and lowering.

or the back of a small project, ⅛ in baltic birch is good enough. I use this thickness for projects 10 in square and smaller and ¼ in thickness for patterns 18 in x 24 in. Larger patterns require the stability provided by ⅜ in backing. The larger the project the thicker the backing board should be.

Other materials that work well for the backing are oak or birch plywood that has a thin veneer on a junk core. Hardboard that is painted white on one side is quite rigid and also makes good backing material, especially since it is about half the price of plywood. If you leave the white side out, it makes an attractive back.

Attaching the Back

The back can be glued on with ordinary white carpenter's glue. Put glue only on the bottom of the pieces. Too much glue oozes to the surface and is difficult to remove.

If you make the back about ⅛ in smaller than the project, there will be a plywood edge showing. This is not attractive and some people paint the plywood edge black. An option is to make the back full size and chamfer the edge. Use a router with ⅜ in rounding-over bit for an edge that looks properly finished.

Spread a small amount of glue on the bottom of the piece only so glue will not ooze out the sides.

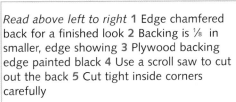

Read above left to right **1** Edge chamfered back for a finished look **2** Backing is ⅛ in smaller, edge showing **3** Plywood backing edge painted black **4** Use a scroll saw to cut out the back **5** Cut tight inside corners carefully

Another way to make a back that works well for simpler projects is to glue the project onto a square back. When the glue dries, set your scroll saw table at an angle 30°- 40° and cut out the back being careful on tight inside corners. Please see my book *The Art of Intarsia* for detailed steps for raising, lowering, and backing.

Finishing

Any finish made for wood will work for intarsia. Finishes come in wax, paste, gel, and liquid forms. They can be sprayed, brushed, wiped, or used for dipping. A variety of lusters is also available. Choose the finish that suits your style and taste.

Usually, three coats on the front and one on the back is sufficient. Be sure to dry well and sand between coats. A vacuum works well to clean off dust between coats. A liquid or spray finish can be applied after the project is glued up. A paste or gel finish should be applied before glue-up because it's difficult to keep the gel out of the grooves.

To preserve the white look of woods such as aspen I use a latex (water) base clear finish applied with spray or brush. Water base finishes raise the wood grain more than oil base finishes do, therefore more sanding between coats is required. Latex finishes also tend to bridge across the space between pieces.

Apply finishes at room temperature (72°F or 22°C). Applying a finish when it's too cold can cause fish eyes, small bubbles, and longer drying time. Fish eyes and runs can also be a problem if the temperature is too warm.

Apply less finish with each coat. I apply finish with about 10 percent thinner for the first coat, then full strength very sparingly for the next coats which helps to reduce runs.

All finishing should be done in a well-ventilated room. Wearing a proper mask will protect from harmful fumes. Finishing allows the artist to be creative. The use of different glosses on the same project adds interest to the work. A high gloss on the eyes of animals and birds adds realism and perspective.

Above Applying paste/gel finish to pieces *Right* Apply final coat full strenght sparingly to help reduce runs

Workshop Safety

Safety is the primary consideration in woodworking. You need to be alert when working with power tools and aware of the potential damage they can inflict. Most tools used in intarsia work are fairly safe, but all tools can inflict harm if you are not careful. Band saws have the potential to inflict injury. One of the most dangerous practices is to clean the table with the band saw running. Wiping your hand across the table absent-mindedly can put your fingers in contact with the blade. So make sure the saw is turned off before you clean up. Cutting small pieces of wood poses another problem. Keep your fingers away from the blade. Keep the wood piece as large as possible as you cut the small pieces off. Use the eraser end of a pencil or a push stick to hold the piece as you make the last cut. A plastic insert with a zero clearance slot will keep the piece from falling into the body of the saw.

Use the eraser end of a pencil to hold small pieces while cutting

Keep work area clean and well ventilated. Wear a safety apron to protect clothing. Short sleeves prevent clothing from being caught in machines.

It is also good practice to unplug the saw when changing blades or a finger could be caught between the wheel and the blade if you accidentally hit the switch. Band saws should be hooked up to a dust collector. The enclosed cabinet of the saw builds pressure because of the spinning wheels and blows dust everywhere. Scroll saws are a safe tool for the most part. They do have a blade that can cut, but you are unlikely to do any serious harm. If a blade breaks, the blade stub can stab you, so be aware of this. Remove your hands from the area and shut the saw off. Also, when cutting thick wood it's possible to get your hand caught as you move the wood under the upper arm when using a parallel arm saw.

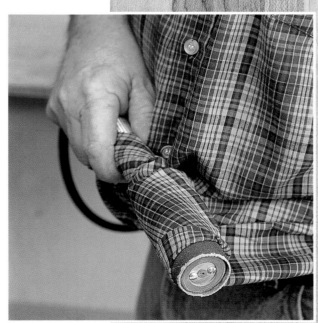

Sanding tools are fairly safe, but ordinary precautions should be taken. These tools can give a nasty abrasive burn. Do not wear loose clothing around spinning drums or small drums that may slip and catch onto clothing, shown at right. If you wear a canvas or leather shop apron you will keep your clothes clean and be less likely to catch your clothing in a tool. Wear eye and ear protection as well.

Please use all tools safely. Read the manuals and follow the manufacturer's instructions. Make sure electrical tools are grounded, and keep all equipment in good repair.

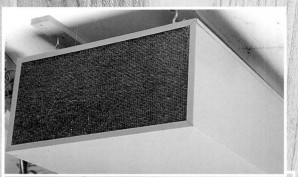

Top 1 An AFD is mounted on the ceiling, has replaceable filters, and cleans the air of the entire shop. Good air filtration removes 99% of fine micro dust *Above* 2 Small portable AFDs are new, don't take up much space, and can be moved from one project to another

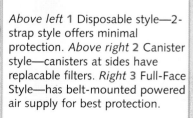

Above left 1 Disposable style—2-strap style offers minimal protection. *Above right* 2 Canister style—canisters at sides have replacable filters. *Right* 3 Full-Face Style—has belt-mounted powered air supply for best protection.

Dust Is Dangerous

In my opinion, the greatest safety hazard in woodworking is the dust that is created and breathed in. It is a serious health risk. Woodworkers should limit their exposure to this dust. Remember, woodworking is a hobby, but breathing isn't. Fine dust particles can cause serious respiratory problems. Man-made woods when cut release chemicals from glues and resins and also cause health problems. Western red cedar releases an allergen called plicatic acid that causes red-cedar asthma. It is wise to protect yourself by having a dust-free working environment. To accomplish this follow these steps.

1 Keep your work area clean.
2 Have all tools hooked up to a dust collector.
3 Use an air filtration device.
4 Wear a good quality dust mask.
5 Don't sand past 220 grit.

For me, the most important tool in my shop is the dust collector. This is an efficient cleaner and all tools can be hooked up to it. Fine dust particles also clog machinery. An air filtration device (AFD) removes airborne dust. Wearing a good quality dust mask is also essential. Masks are rated according to their efficiency. Purchase one that gives the protection you need.
Dust collectors are essential for any serious woodcrafter. They come in four basic forms.

1 Shop vacuums pick up large debris pieces from floor and workbench but are not as effective for fine dust.
2 Portable dust collectors temporarily hook up to each tool. Dedicated dust collectors set up to each tool permanently with ducts. Chips and dust are drawn through a blower fan into collection bags that are fine enough to keep small particles from escaping into the air. Bags should have a 1-micron or finer rating. A remote on and off switch makes it easier to use this collector. Small portable AFDs have the advantage of being able to be moved from one project area to another, but are no substitute for a proper dust collection system
3 Permanently mounted AFDs are mounted on the ceiling and are very effective in removing airborne dust. Filters should have a 1-micron rating. A remote on and off switch makes it easier to use the collector.
4 A downdraft table is a recent development in dust control and expensive to purchase but inexpensive and easy to make. Use a table with a 6-8 in space put under vacuum. Holes in the tabletop allow dust to be sucked down and away from you as you sand. The vacuum can be provided by hooking it up to a dust collector as shown or use a furnace squirrel cage to blow dust outside. To order plans see p 96.

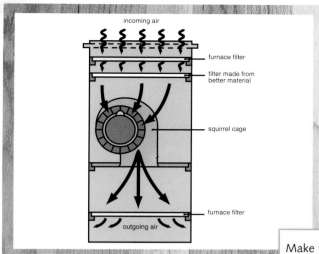

incoming air

furnace filter

filter made from better material

squirrel cage

furnace filter

outgoing air

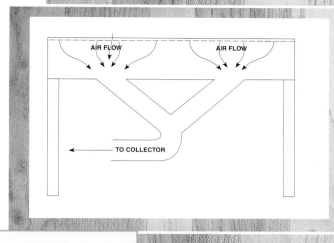

AIR FLOW   AIR FLOW

TO COLLECTOR

Make your own downdraft table

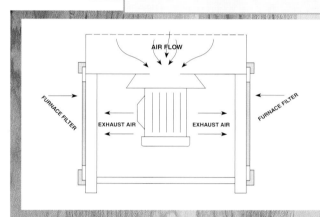

AIR FLOW

FURNACE FILTER

EXHAUST AIR   EXHAUST AIR

FURNACE FILTER

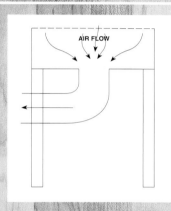

AIR FLOW

Dust Collection Challenges

One advantage of shaping and sanding your woodworking pieces by hand is that less dust is thrown into the air. Sandpaper, files, rasps, and tools such as the Detail sander do not create as much dust as power sanders. Any type of sander that has a wheel turning at a high speed will throw dust into the air and it is difficult to control with a dust collection port.

You will probably have to make your own dust collection port in order to accommodate your own particular dust-creating circumstances, as I have done for my flap sander.

Small pneumatic sanders present an unusual problem. Used in a power carver or flex shaft they are not stationary and therefore more difficult to collect from. Something as simple as attaching a dust hose to your sleeve will work. I am now working on a dust-free sanding cabinet for use with small sanders.

Above left Dust collector hooked to sanding tools
Above right Dust collector hose attached to sleeve

Wood Colors

Cedar comes in a variety of shades. This example shows samples of each wood unfinished and finished

The intarsia artist chooses his palette of colors from the variety of wood hues available. Selecting the wood is the most personal part of artistic creation and the individuality of the intarsia project depends not only on wood colors but also grain and wood type. It is important to remember that colors can vary within a species, and grain textures add richness and shading. Learning about different woods and knowing which wood is best for each project can be a lifelong learning experience. For example, heartwood can be a different color than sapwood in some species. Grain textures can vary depending on how the log is cut—is it quarter sawn or flat sawn? The way you use the wood and blend it with other woods will greatly affect the outcome of your project. Although some of the woods are expensive, not much is required for a project so the overall expense is not great.

The most common wood used in intarsia work is western red cedar. Names of woods can vary and western red cedar is known as shinglewood, Idaho cedar, stinking cedar, canoe wood, and pacific red cedar in different areas. This wood is easy to cut and shape, readily available, and not too expensive. It has the greatest variety of shades and grain textures that I have found. However, some shades are often difficult to find, especially dark western red cedar. If you can't find what you need try the darkening method on this page.

WOOD COLOR LIST
The intarsia artist has a great palette of wood colors to work with to create any project. A great choice of wood is available from sawmills, lumberyards, specialty stores, and mail order through specialty magazines. Even a walk through the woods can yield unusual fallen pieces for a variety of grains and colors.

RED
Bloodwood (called pau rainha, satine urbane, cardinal wood, muirapirange, Brazil redwood, or palo de sangre) is my first choice for a deep rich red color. This wood is very hard and difficult to cut. Use a #9 or #12 precision ground style scroll saw blade or a band saw, which will handle it best by far. Expensive, but available through specialty hardwood stores.
Aromatic cedar (called red cedar, Tennessee cedar, chest cedar, or eastern red cedar) has a unique odor, very aromatic. Used mainly to line closets and chests because its aroma repels moths. It is soft and easy to cut. The oil content can make it somewhat difficult to finish (try non-yellowing finish or a latex water base finish). Color ranges from a pinkish red to dark red

HOW TO DARKEN WESTERN RED CEDAR

Dark western red cedar is sometimes difficult to find. A tip passed on to me by David Seaman of British Columbia, Canada will help you overcome this problem. You can darken light cedar quite easily. Place rusted metal in water along with 2 cups of coarse rock salt and submerge light western red cedar boards in this solution. Place some of the rusted metal between the boards to hasten the process. Stir the water once in a while to stir up rust. It takes about 4-6 weeks for the dark color to penetrate the wood to a depth of ¼ in to ⅜ in. Remove the boards and allow to dry at room temperature for another 4-6 weeks. Once you cut out the pieces and do the shaping, submerge them in the solution again overnight if the shaping exposes some lighter wood. This process gives a natural looking dark color that does not look stained.

If you keep a batch processing all the time you will soon have a supply of dark cedar. One drawback to this process is that the wood is soft and easily dented or scratched, so needs to be handled carefully.

Note   Cedar can cause allergies known as red cedar asthma, so using it can be dangerous. Some kind of mask protection is recommended.

with streaks of white. May be difficult to find in wide boards. Cracks easily because of internal stress but has lots of interesting knots. Readily available and moderately priced.

BLACK

Black walnut (dark brown to rich dark black) is moderately hard, moderately priced, and easy to find.

Wenge (called fiboto, dikela, or pallissandre) is very hard, very black, but can have brown streaks throughout. Expensive and difficult to find in some areas.

South American walnut (part of juglans species, similar to North American walnut) is softer than our walnut but cuts and sands well. Provides good contrast black. Expensive, fairly easy to find.

WHITE

Aspen (member of the cottonwood family, also known as poplar) is my first choice for white. It is easy to find and not expensive. Look through lumber piles to find the whitest boards.

Spruce (called Adirondack spruce, blue spruce, or skunk spruce) is easy to cut and sand. Various shades of white, creamy white, and can have gray or blue streaks.

Pine (soft white or harder yellowpine) is similar to spruce. Easy to work. White or can have bluish streak.

Silver maple (called Mississippi maple or shimmering maple) is harder than other white woods. Can have pinkish or brown streaks through it or can be found very white with a grain that gives a shimmering effect.

GREEN

Poplar (the heartwood of this species can be green or a gray color) is very common and boards often have a green cast. It is easy to work, easy to find, and not too expensive.

Sumac (called staghorn sumac or velvet sumac) is unavailable as a commercial wood. You will have to find your own source in northeastern United States, eastern Canada and some areas in the West such as the interior of British Columbia and northwest U.S.A. This small tree is rarely over five inches in diameter. It has a distinctive green color and is easy to work. I resaw it into small boards and glue it onto some scrap to get the thickness I need.

Vera wood (called lignum-vitae, maracalbo, guyacan, or bera cuchivaro) is a hard waxy wood with a nice green color when worked. Difficult to find and expensive.

YELLOW

Pau amarillo (called Brazilian satinwood or satina) is my first choice for its beautiful yellow color and easy working qualities. Expensive. Available through most specialty hardwood stores.

Yellow cedar (provides a nice contrast to pau amarillo). This pale yellow wood is readily available, soft and easy to work, and moderately priced. The figure and grain are not spectacular.

Other woods such as hickory, ponderosa pine, and caragana have a

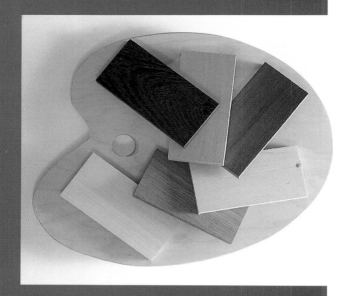

pale yellow hue and are good used for contrast. Hickory and pine are easy to find. Caragana is used extensively as a shelter belt tree in the West or grown as an ornamental tree in urban yards, and is not readily available unless you can harvest it from the tree.

PURPLE

Purple heart (called pauroxo, violet wood, and coracy) is difficult to cut and shape. It will burn easily when sanding with power tools, so stop frequently to allow it to cool. Begin with coarse sandpaper. Easy to find but expensive. Keep it on hand for color and interest.

ORANGE

African padauk (called corail, yomo, barwood, vermillion, African coral wood, muenga, bois rouge, and comwood) is another of my favorite woods. Easy to cut and shape, it has an intoxicating smell when worked. Color can vary from orange to blood red. Readily available and moderately priced.

Orange osage is a hardwood that is fairly easy to work. Bright yellow when first worked, it will turn orangy brown when exposed to light. Easy to find and reasonably priced.

BLUE GRAY

Spruce/Pine can have streaks of gray or blue color. Look for these boards in piles of inexpensive fence boards at the lumber yard. I have found this the best source of a blue color. It's worth looking through the pile of boards.

Mahogany with a nice silver gray color can be found in a search of lumberyard mahogany boards. A latex finish is the best way to preserve this gray color.

Special Effects Woods

Zebrawood is pale brown with dark streaks. Easy to work. Available from specialty stores but very expensive.

Red gum can have contrasting shades of brown, red, and black within one board. Beautiful grain in the form of a ribbon stripe

Willow can have contrasting shades similar to red gum. Also beautiful.

Bird's-eye maple has little round knot swirls that can be used effectively for some projects.

Lacewood has a beautiful lacy look. Wood ranges from light pink to reddish brown with a silvery sheen.

Sycamore (called water beech, button ball, buttonwood, planetree, or ghost wood because its white bark is mottled with shades of green and brown). Boards can be reddish brown or flesh color, ¼ sawn boards can have a mottled texture. Moderately hard, readily available, not too expensive.

Figured cherry (called rum cherry, whiskey cherry or wild cherry. Moderately hard to work, burns easily, finishes very nice. Readily available and reasonably priced.

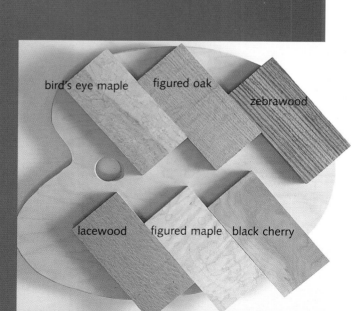

bird's eye maple   figured oak

zebrawood

lacewood   figured maple   black cherry

Spalted basswood (called yellow basswood, black limetree, beetree, linden, whitewood, or wickup). White, spalts easily, dark streaks thoughout. Soft, easy to cut and shape. Readily available, not too expensive.

Unusual Woods

Spalted woods have dark lines caused by fungus and molds that have grown in the tree veins after it dies. Woods such as birch, maple, basswood, and oak often can be found spalted.

Burls are found in a number of species. These wartlike growths on the trees are caused by some trauma to the tree such as a lightning strike. The wood in these burls is interesting and ideal for intarsia. Redwood, cedar, and birch burl slabs are fairly common.

Palm is unique in appearance and is actually a grass.

Composite beam is man-made from wood chips, so is not a particular tree species. It is used for structural beams in buildings. It presents different looks depending on how it is cut.

Aspenite is another man-made material that can look like sand or a forest floor.

The choice of wood is almost endless. The more you learn about the different species the more flexibility you will have in making your projects. Some woods used in intarsia are expensive, but because you don't need large amounts, they are more affordable. A couple of board feet will go a long way in making your project.

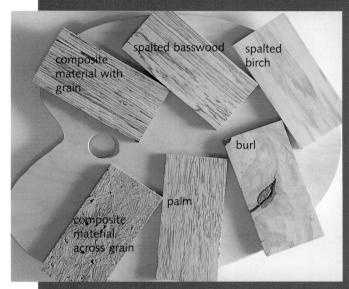

composite material with grain

spalted basswood

spalted birch

burl

palm

composite material across grain

Consult these books for further information about wood

Know Your Woods, Albert Constantine Jr., Charles Scribner's Sons, New York (revised 1975).

A Guide to Useful Woods of the World, (James H. Flynn co-editor) Forest Products Society, of Madison, Wisconsin.

World Woods in Color, William Alexander Lincoln,. Linden Publishing Co.

TIPS FOR WOOD USE

1 Make sure wood is dry before you use it or it may crack or check, glue may fail, or the finish will bubble. Moisture content shouldn't be above 8% for safe use. Most commercially kiln-dried wood is around 18%, so must be dried. You can dry it in your own shop in small quantities.

2 Dry small green pieces in your workshop. Stack larger pieces 6 in off the floor with ¾ in stickers between the boards and away from a wall for good circulation. When stacked inside, green wood will dry more rapidly. Paint the ends of the boards to prevent end checking.

3 Large pieces can be stacked outdoors off the ground with ¾ in stickers between the boards. Cover the pile and add some weight to help prevent warping. Paint the ends of the boards to prevent checking.

4 One-inch material that has been stored indoors for 6 months or more will be dry enough to use. Small pieces will dry quickly.

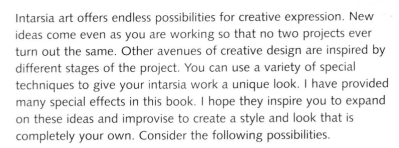

Being Creative

Intarsia art offers endless possibilities for creative expression. New ideas come even as you are working so that no two projects ever turn out the same. Other avenues of creative design are inspired by different stages of the project. You can use a variety of special techniques to give your intarsia work a unique look. I have provided many special effects in this book. I hope they inspire you to expand on these ideas and improvise to create a style and look that is completely your own. Consider the following possibilities.

Special Effects for Projects

Carving details with various tools, wood burning, sandblasting, wire brushing, burnishing, flap sander technique, and leather stamps will give your work a special look.

Staining and Painting

Staining and painting the pieces is another way to be creative. This technique is a good option for people who have trouble finding all the different woods suggested in some patterns. It is also a chance to be creative in combining stained pieces with painted pieces and natural wood pieces.

Nondirectional Intarsia

This technique eliminates all the problems associated with fitting the pieces of an intarsia project because the entire pattern is traced on and cut from one piece of wood. You can even use MDF board, a man-made material from pressed sawdust. Because this technique requires that the project be painted, grain direction is not important when cutting. Having no cutting or fitting problems greatly simplifies project building. MDF shapes and sands easily, and turns out some satisfying objects.

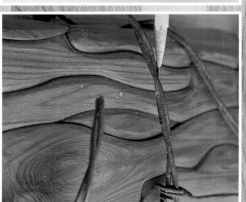

Read from top **1** Use plexiglass to enhance intarsia projects **2** Painting and staining wood is an option **3** Brass screws add authentisicty to porthole scene **4** A freestanding project expands the use of intarsia **5** Rusty barbed wire wrapped around a project creates realism **6** An intarsia piggy bank is a fun and functional project

Freestanding

This technique allows you to make an intarsia project that stands independently, like a sculpture. I like this technique because it expands the look and uses for intarsia

Enhanced 3-D

This method adds more perspective to a project. Dowels are used to make parts of a project stand out from the main part of the project. This has a very startling effect on the over-all presentation.

Different Materials

As you work you will find yourself thinking of various ways to make your projects different. You can incorporate materials such as acrylic, glass, and metal for special effects. Natural materials such as rocks, sand, barn boards, or an old fence post can be used to create a different look. All or any of these can be used as your imagination dictates. For example, wrapping some rusty barbed wire around an old fence post that you have used in the design would make it look more authentic and be very creative. Acrylics are another source of inspiration. This material comes in all colors, cuts easily with a scroll saw, and can be made to look like the glass in a stained glass window. Or you can turn an intarsia piece into a mirror with the use of glass. Brass and aluminium can both be cut with a scroll saw using a jeweler blade. Either metal can be used to add interest to a project. If you are one of those people who like to make functional things, most intarsia pieces can be turned into frames for clocks or made into mirrors or fancy picture frames. They can even be made into piggy banks.

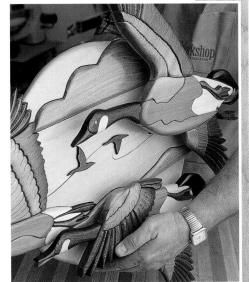

Read from the top
1 This fish is made from MDF. Half is painted, half is unpainted **2** Intarsia can incorporate a clock **3** Dowels are used to make the geese stand out from the project to give a realistic effect **4** Natural materials such as rocks, sand, and twigs are used in this project **5** This intarsia loon becomes a mirror with the addition of glass in the design

Intarsia Projects

Moonflight

Goose #1

Suggested shades of wood

■	Black walnut or very dark WRC
□	White aspen
▨	Medium WRC
▨	Medium dark WRC
▨	Dark WRC
▨	Light WRC

Goose #1

Suggested raising and lowering

▨	No change in level
▨	L
▨	R

Moonflight

This is one of my favorite projects. When it hangs on the wall a draft from an opened door causes air movement and the geese move, giving the appearance of flight. This project is called enhanced 3-D because two of the birds extend beyond the base on dowels creating a realistic animated appearance. I suggest pau amarillo for the moon because of its rich yellow color.

No. of pieces - 107
Finished size - 27 in x 27 in

Wood needed
Yellow pau amarillo – 8 in x 30 in
Black walnut or very dark western red cedar (WRC) – 6 in x 12 in
White aspen – 6 in x 6 in
Medium dark WRC – 6 in x 12 in
Medium WRC – 6 in x 24 in
Light WRC – 6 in x 6 in
Dark WRC – 12 in x 12 in

1 Enlarge (p10) patterns on pages 30, 32, 33 to the desired size.
2 Choose wood shades or types as pattern suggests, and transfer (p10) pattern to ¾ in thick wood.
3 This project contains 3 individual projects that come together at the finish. To assist reassembly for shaping and gluing it is helpful to mark the pattern pieces and the matching pieces on the wood. Transfer the mark on the central piece to the bottom of the piece as you begin shaping. To make fitting easier cut out the pieces carefully, making sure the saw blade is square to the table (p11). Pieces won't fit if the edges are at an angle.
4 Once pieces are cut out, assemble the project and check for fit.
5 Raise and lower (p13) pieces as the pattern suggests. To make the pau amarillo thinner resaw it using a band saw with a Swedish silicon steel blade.
6 Reassemble the project and draw reference lines (p14).
7 Shape the pieces to the reference lines. Shape the birds so they look realistic. The birds should have a rounded shape. Check to see that you achieve a smooth transition from one level to the next.
8 When shaping is finished, sand all the pieces by hand or with a flap sander or star twister sander. I don't sand past 220 grit.
9 Add detail to the feathers with a wood-burning tool (see opposite p). This will add interest to the look of the bird. A wood burner is a

good investment for an intarsia artist, but if you don't have one you could use a fine tipped felt pen.

10 To make eyes use a ¼ in dowel of white aspen or other light wood. Drill a hole to fit the dowel. Glue in place. Sand smooth.

11 Reassemble the pieces on the backing material (¼ in plywood 30 in x 30 in) and trace around each of them. Cut out.

12 Glue the pieces to the cut out backs using white carpenter's glue.

13 When the glue has dried (30 minutes to 1 hour), drill the holes in the moon part, as marked, and on the backs of the two geese, as marked to match the dowels – the smaller the dowels the more movement the geese will make. Make 3 small silhouette geese to glue to moon.

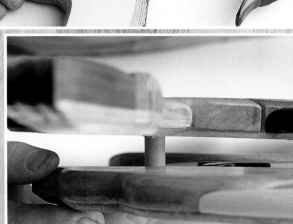

14 Apply the finish of your choice at this time (p16).

15 Glue the dowels to the back of the geese and then to the moon. The glue will give you 10 minutes to adjust the position. Try hanging the piece on the wall and move the geese to fly upward. If the hole is too big or in the wrong place, glue a stub piece of dowel in the hole and allow to dry. Redrill hole in a new location. To hang, find center point and place hanger on back.

Note
Attach goose #1 and goose #2 at marks on moon pattern. Drill ⅜ in hole ⅜ in deep. Find balance point on geese and drill ⅜ in hole ⅜ in deep. Use 1¼ in long dowel for goose #1 and 1¾ in long dowel for goose #2. Glue in place where marked on pattern.

Read from top **1** Shows back of birds with dowels **2** Shows moon with holes for dowels **3** Side view shows how birds are attached **4** Wood burning the feathers **5** Close-up of finished feathers using wood-burning tool

direction of
wood grain

slope down

◯ indicates open space

Goose #1

Goose #2

Goose #3

Suggested shades of wood

Black walnut	Medium dark WRC
White aspen	Dark WRC
Medium WRC	

Suggested shades of wood

Black walnut	Medium dark WRC
White aspen	Dark WRC
Medium WRC	Yellow pau amarillo or Yellow cedar
Light WRC	

Goose #2

Suggested raising and lowering

No change in level	
L	
R	

Suggested raising and lowering

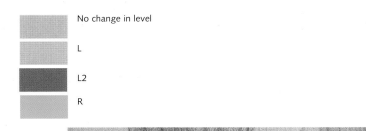

No change in level	
L	
L2	
R	

Goose #2

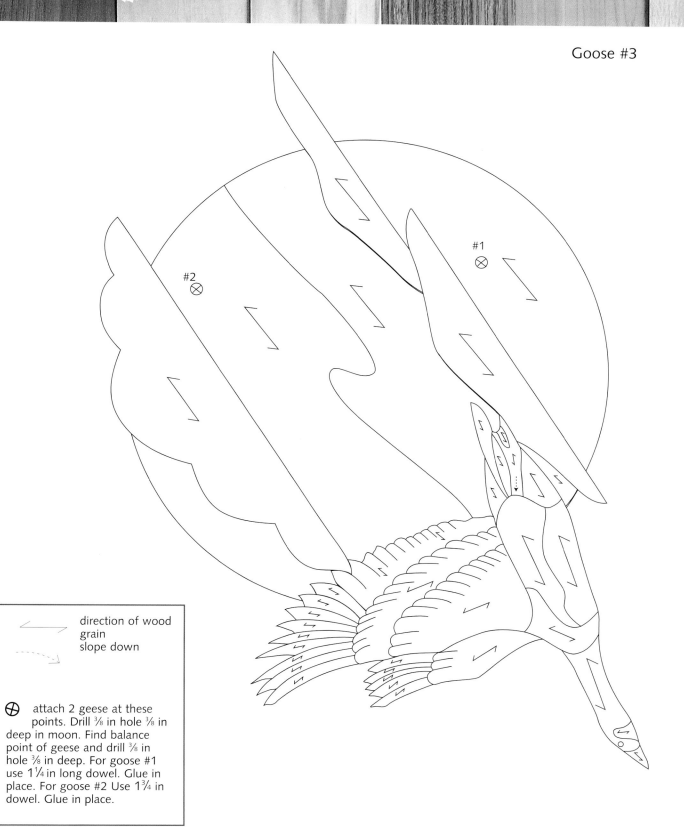

direction of wood
grain
slope down

⊕ attach 2 geese at these
    points. Drill ⅜ in hole ⅜ in
deep in moon. Find balance
point of geese and drill ⅜ in
hole ⅜ in deep. For goose #1
use 1¼ in long dowel. Glue in
place. For goose #2 Use 1¾ in
dowel. Glue in place.

Rearing Horse

Rearing Horse

This rearing horse can hang on the wall as a regular intarsia project or it can stand alone by modifying the three pieces that form the ground in front of the horse to become a base. The walnut and cedar woods give the horse a traditional look. To add realism try to make the wood horse body look like hair with a special effects technique using a wire brush, shown at right.

No. of pieces - 30
Finished size - 18 in x 12 in

Wood needed
Black walnut or very dark western red cedar (WRC) – 1 in x 4 in
Dark WRC – 4 in x 24 in
Light WRC – 2 in x 8 in
Medium WRC – 5 ½ in x 24 in

1 Enlarge (p10) pattern on page 37 to the desired size.

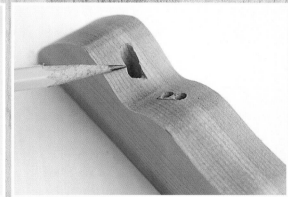

2 Choose wood shades or types as the pattern suggests and transfer (p10) the pattern to ¾ in thick wood.

3 Using the saw of your choice square the blade to the table (p11) and cut out all the pattern pieces on the line.

4 Assemble pattern pieces and check for fit. Pieces should fit together as closely as possible. A kerf saw width (¹⁄₁₆ in) between pieces is acceptable.

5 Raise and lower (p13) pieces as the pattern suggests.

6 Reassemble the pattern and mark reference lines (p14) to aid shaping, using reference lines as a guide.

7 Shape the pieces and make a smooth transition from one level to the next. Try to avoid flat edges. Shaping is very important to the finished look of the project.

8 To add realism to the horse attach a wire wheel to a flex shaft and lightly work the wire brush over the surface of the wood. This technique is speeded up by dampening the wood. Make the wire brush strokes in the direction of how the hair would be on a horse. Practice the technique on scrap wood before you try it on the project. Wear a glove on the hand you use to hold the wood. Painful scrapes may result if the brush runs up the wood onto your hand.

9 To make the wall hanging cut out the pattern, as shown, and do not make the base. Cut off the plywood backing at the dotted line on the pattern. The 3 base pieces shown above, are for the standing horse. The 3

Above left **1** Base pieces for rearing horse
Above right **2** Hole for leaves *Above* **3** Screws secure horse to base

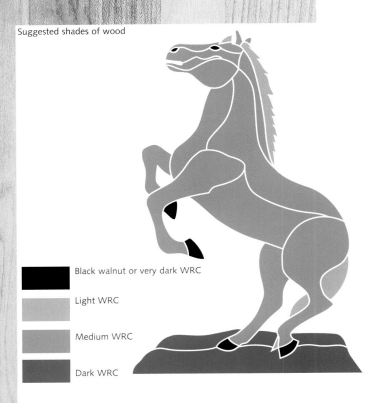

Suggested shades of wood

⬛	Black walnut or very dark WRC
⬜	Light WRC
⬜	Medium WRC
⬜	Dark WRC

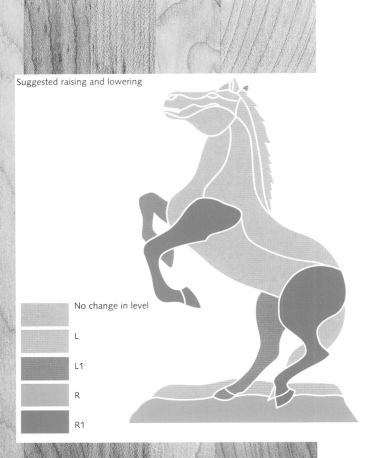

Suggested raising and lowering

⬜	No change in level
⬜	L
⬜	L1
⬜	R
⬜	R1

pieces representing the rocks are shaped and glued together on top of the base piece. Make the leaves from ⅛ in strips of wood and cut them to shape. Drill three ⅛ in holes ½ in deep in a line, as shown p35, to hold the leaves. Move the drill back and forth between the holes to create an oblong hole for the leaves.

10 *Optional step* I brushed the base pieces with a torch and gave the base an earth look. It is safer to do the torching outside but if you do it inside be sure to have a fire extinguisher on hand. Do the burning on a steel surface (garbage can lid p40) and burn only 2 pieces at a time. Be sure the wood does not catch fire: if it does, blow it out by mouth immediately. Move the torch back and forth over the piece to darken it gradually.

11 Sand the pieces using a flap sander or a star twister with 220 grit paper or sand by hand.

12 Cut out the horse backing from ¼ in x 12 in x 8 in plywood.

13 Make the horse shown on the pattern.

14 To make a wall hanging omit the free-standing base pieces and cut ground piece only.

15 For freestanding project extend the ground piece in front of the horse 3 in to fit on the base pattern. Cut base from ¼ in plywood. Area behind dotted lines remains the same.

16 Attach the horse to the base with wood screws, p 35.

17 Glue the base pieces to the base and trim them if needed.

18 Apply the finish of your choice (p16).

1 *Above* base pieces preassembled and finished

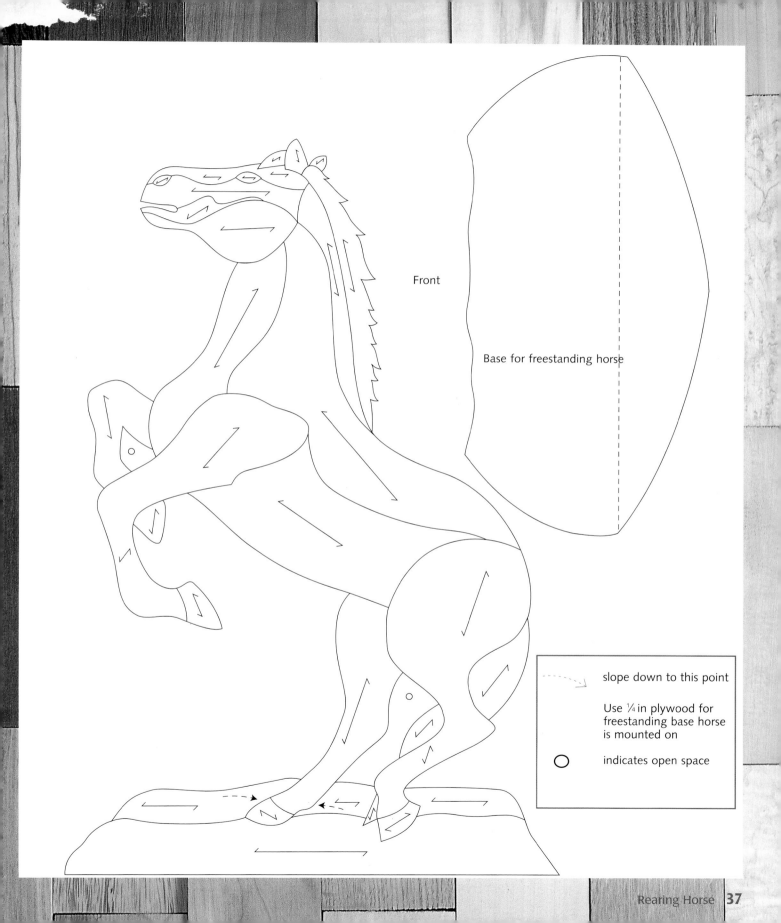

Front

Base for freestanding horse

slope down to this point

Use ¼ in plywood for freestanding base horse is mounted on

indicates open space

Thunderbird

Thunderbird

The splendid art of the Coastal Indians of the Pacific Northwest reflects their rich culture and history. Myths and legends, rich in the symbolism that defines Haida art, tell us about the life of a people who place great importance on their interaction with nature in all its forms. I have always admired this art and it is with respect that I offer this tribute to its greatness. I have utilized the thunderbird that was responsible for thunder and lightning in Haida culture and the killer whale, long regarded as the greatest living thing. This striking intarsia project combines a number of different woodworking techniques and special effects.

No. of pieces - 27
Finished size - 18 in x 12 in

Wood needed
Light western red cedar (WRC) - 2 in x 6 in
Medium WRC - 4 in x 8 in
Medium dark WRC - 3 in x 8 in
Pine (to paint) - 5 fl in x 18 in
White aspen - 6 in x 24 in

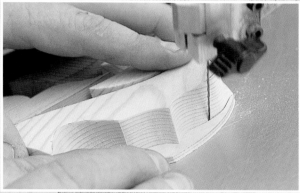

1 Enlarge (p10) pattern on page 42 to the desired size.
2 Choose wood shades or types as the pattern suggests and transfer (p10) the pattern to ¾ in thick wood. Be sure to trace with the pencil held at an angle. Tracing with the pencil held straight up will make the pieces larger and can cause fitting problems. Be aware of wood grain and the matching and balancing of wood shades.
3 Cut out the pieces carefully right on the line, making sure the saw blade is square to the table (p11).
4 Number the bottom of the cut out pieces to match the numbers that you put on the pattern.
5 Assemble the pieces and check for fit (within a saw kerf or ¹⁄₁₆ in is

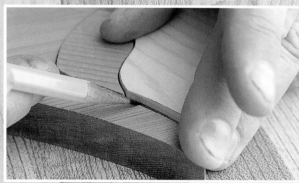

acceptable, but anything more than that will change the shape of the entire piece). To make sure that pieces fit hold two pieces tightly together and run a scroll saw blade between them where they touch (p12).

6 You can glue all the pieces to be raised the same thickness to a common board (p14). Set the saw at an angle and cut out around the pieces.

1 *Top* Resawing the piece thinner 2 Sawing out raised pieces with saw at an angle 3 Assemble and draw reference lines for shaping 4 *Left* Shaping with a Sandstorm sander 5 *Right* Sanding with a flap sander

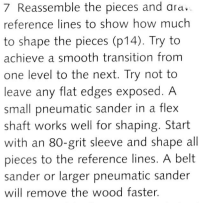

7 Reassemble the pieces and draw reference lines to show how much to shape the pieces (p14). Try to achieve a smooth transition from one level to the next. Try not to leave any flat edges exposed. A small pneumatic sander in a flex shaft works well for shaping. Start with an 80-grit sleeve and shape all pieces to the reference lines. A belt sander or larger pneumatic sander will remove the wood faster.

8 Reassemble the project and check the transition. Sand all pieces with a 120-grit sleeve.

9 Some pieces in the project are textured. The texturing is done with a small propane torch (left). Burn the wood until the surface is charred (it looks cracked). Move the torch back and forth and distribute the heat so the wood won't actually catch fire. Cool the wood. The torch burns out the soft part of the grain and makes texturing easier. A wire brush will also take out the soft part of the grain.

10 Continue texturing with a flap sander or star twister sander with coarse paper.

11 Sand all pieces with a flap sander or a star twister with fine grit strips. I do not sand past 220 grit.

12 I use ¼ in Baltic birch for the backing board, but ¼ in oak or birch plywood is also acceptable.

13 Then assemble the project on the backing material, trace around it, and cut out the backing.

14 Painting is done at this stage. Paint the pieces

Reading from top left to right **1** Backing meets the edge and is chamfered **2** Backing is set back from the edge **3** Torching a piece **4** Texturing on a flap sander **5** Texturing on a star twister

...owing the suggestions at right. Paint them a solid color or allow the paint to set for a few seconds and wipe it off for a stained look. Finish all natural pieces with a clear varnish. Allow to dry.

15 Assemble pieces on the cut out backing board and begin gluing, one piece at a time, working around the outside to form a frame to hold the other pieces in place. Use ordinary white carpenter's glue. Do not put glue on the edge of pieces. Allow to dry.

16 There are 2 ways to finish the back—bring the back to the edge of the material and chamfer the back (p40). Cut on the line for this method with a #3 or #5 double tooth reverse blade or make the back smaller than the project by cutting ⅛ in inside the line (see p40).

17 Chamfer the back by using a sander or router with a ¼ in rounding overbit.

18 Attach a hanger to the back to hang the project on the wall.

Note An alternative way to make the backing is to cut a backing board larger than the project and glue the pieces to it (p15). Allow to dry. Set the scroll saw table at a 30 - 40° angle and cut out. This allows you to cut out and chamfer at the same time.

Suggested shades of wood

⬛	Black walnut or very dark WRC or black painted pine
⬜	White aspen
🟫	Painted Pine or bloodwood

⬛	Medium dark WRC
⬛	Medium WRC
⬛	Light WRC

All textured pieces are pine painted red or you can use untextured red bloodwood

Suggested raising and lowering

⬜	No change in level
🟦	L1
	Open space

⬜	R
🟫	R1
🟫	R2

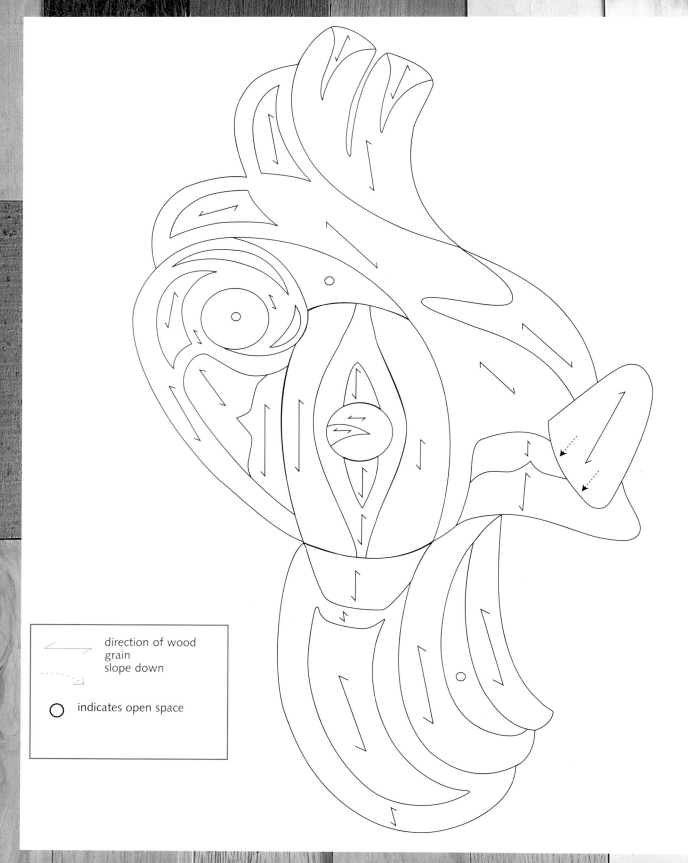

direction of wood
grain
slope down

◯ indicates open space

Nativity Scene

Twig Stable or Wood Stable

Nativity Scene **43**

Suggested shades of wood

Dark WRC

White aspen

Yellow pau amarillo

Medium dark WRC

Light WRC

Medium WRC

Suggested raising and lowering

No change in level
Figures are rounded individuallly

Nativity Scene

This challenging intarsia project is freestanding and makes use of natural materials – rock, sand, and twigs. It utilizes texturing techniques to add interest and has a removable back for easy storage. The first project I made was for a friend who wanted a setting to display a collection of porcelain nativity figurines. The next one I made for myself and it has a set of figurines made from wood. It has become a tradition in my family to set out this piece every year. We assemble the nativity scene at the beginning of the Christmas season. The piece is now a treasured family heirloom.

No. of pieces - 83
Finished size - 20 in x 16 in

Wood needed
Light western red cedar (WRC) – 6 in x 30 in
Medium dark WRC – 6 in x 12 in
Dark WRC – 6 in x 24 in
Black walnut or very dark WRC – 6 in x 20 in
Yellow cedar or yellow pine – 6 in x 6 in
Yellow pau amarillo – 6 in x 12 in
White aspen – 6 in x 6 in
White aspen for sheep – 1 ½ in x 2 in x 10 in long
Dark WRC for stable – 8 in x 36 in
Dowels – ⅛ in x 48 in long; ⅛ in x 30 in long
Scrap wood – pieces left over for figurines
Plywood (¼ in) – 20 in x 40 in

1 Enlarge (p10) the patterns on pages 48, 49, 50, 51, 52 to the desired size.
2 Choose wood shades or types as the pattern suggests and transfer (p10) the pattern to ¾ in thick wood.
3 Using the saw of your choice, make sure the blade is square to the table (p11), and cut out the pieces carefully.
4 To make the matching palm leaves I inlaid darker V pieces. Cut out the leaves, cut in the notch, and trace the notch with a pencil onto the dark wood. Then cut outside the line and trim the notch pieces to fit the notch in the leaves. Glue in the dark pieces and shape the leaves as one piece.
5 Match the pieces to the pattern with numbers which helps with assembly or if the pieces fall to the floor.
6 Once all the pieces for the upright setting are cut out, assemble everything and check for fit. If they are too wide, make the base bigger to match the backing material. If the measurement is only slightly off I try to accommodate it.

7 Raise and lower the pieces as the pattern suggests.

8 Reassemble the project and draw reference lines to aid in shaping the pieces. Try to achieve a smooth transition between levels and avoid flat edges unless they are part of the design.

9 The figurines are shaped on both sides and don't have a backing board.

10 Sand all the pieces up to 220 grit.

11 Reassemble the pieces on the ¼ in plywood 20 in x 40 in backing board, trace around them, and cut out the backing. Make sure you leave room at the bottom of the backing board to attach it to the base, as shown in the pattern.

12 Glue pieces and backing with ordinary white carpenter's glue.

13 Make the base from ¼ in Baltic birch or ordinary birch plywood, being sure to match the background.

14 Make a frame under the base (illus #3 on pattern) from ¾ in pine or cedar. The front board is 5 ¼ in wide to allow for trimming the front round. (The other boards are 3 in wide and cut to fit). Glue and clamp these boards in place.

15 Drill ⅜ in holes for the fence posts, as marked on the pattern.

16 Posts are ⅜ in x ⅜ in x 2 ⅞ in long (illus #2 on pattern) and made from dark western red cedar (twigs could also be used). I use ⅛ in dowels for the rails (6 at 8 in long and 3 at 10 in long). Drill holes in the posts where indicated for the rails (illus #1 on pattern). It is easier to fit the rails by drilling the holes in the center posts one size larger. Notch the post up ⅜ in from the bottom to use as reference marks and sand the bottom of the post round with a wood file. Leave them a bit tight for the holes so they can be driven in for a tight fit. Sand some post irregularities so they will look hand hewn. Assemble each section of fence and drive it in place. Glue should not be required. Fence posts are dark western red cedar.

17 Stable can be constructed of wood or made of twigs. Use ½ in thick dark western red cedar for the roof and medium western red cedar for the walls.

Wood Stable

a) Cut out the back from the template without the door opening but with the notches cut out for the rafters. Cut out the front from the template with the door opening and notches cut out for the rafter timbers.

Above Assemble the pieces for the figures *Below* Apply glue sparingly

Below Remove the back for easy storage

> Ridge timber
> ⅜ in x ⅜ in x 6 ⅝ in long
> ⅜ in x ⅜ in x 6 in long
> ⅜ in x ⅜ in x 5 ¼ in long

b) Cut out the stable sides 3 ½ in x 4 in with the window, as shown on the pattern.

c) Glue and clamp the sides, front, and back together. Sand the sides on a belt sander to get smooth joints.

d) Glue on the roof boards and trim them at an angle to match the front peak.

e) Make the bottom of the stable from ½ in plywood. Use contact glue and adhere it to stable.

Twig Stable

a) Assemble the twigs on MDF base, as shown on p47.

b) Drill holes to fit the twigs you find.

c) Cut four fairly straight twigs ⅝ in to ¾ in diameter and 5 in long. Stand them in the holes. Try for a snug fit.

d) With the twigs you have collected from dead branches, build a free form stable, using the photo as a guide. Glue or nail the twigs in place as required. Glue on the roof.

18 Baby Cradle can also be made of twigs. Use a twig 1 in diameter and 2 in long. Cut ¼ in from each end, scroll out center, and glue the ends back on. Find two dry barked twigs for cradle legs, cut them to shape, and glue on. Or use pattern p48.

Above Stable may be constructed of twigs or cedar
Below Baby cradle may be constructed from twigs or cedar

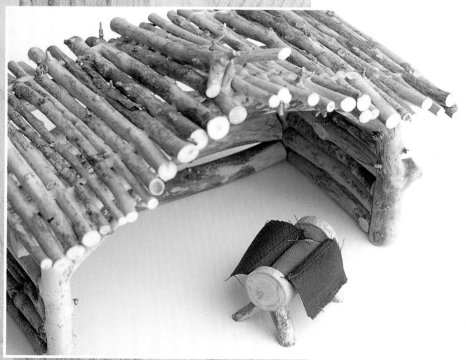

19 Rocks (1 in - 1 ½ in) are represented by pebbles. Use pebbles with flat bottom or sand them flat with a coarse belt or a 6 in belt sander. Position the stable and place the rocks. Glue in place with white carpenter's glue.

20 Sand is applied within the dotted line (see pattern). Spread white carpenter's glue and sprinkle on the sand.

21 Nativity figures are freestanding intarsia, but they do not have a backing board to hold them together. Spend extra time to get the pieces to fit well together because glue is placed only where pieces touch during glue-up. Pieces have rounded edges on both sides to define their shape but don't have a lot of shaping. The pieces are small and shaped by hand with 120 grit sandpaper. Glue with ordinary white carpenter's glue. Allow to dry. Sand bottoms on a belt sander.

22 Apply the finish of your choice to the

project. Use a latex water-base spray-on finish for rocks and sand. This also helps to hold them in place.

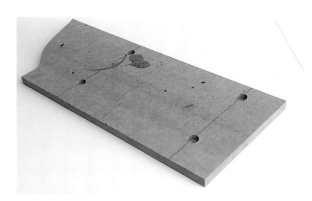

Top 1 Assemble the twig stable on MDF base and drill holes for main posts *Center* 2 Place completed stable on base lining up with holes *Bottom* 3 Round twigs to fit in holes

Suggested shades of wood

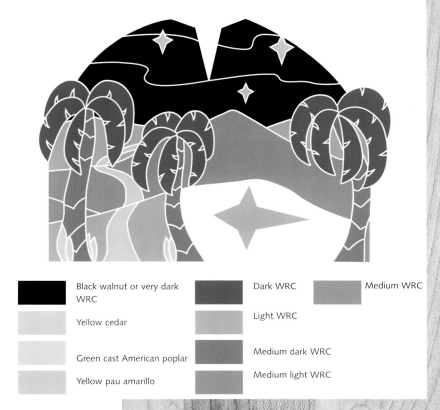

Black walnut or very dark WRC		Dark WRC		Medium WRC
Yellow cedar		Light WRC		
Green cast American poplar		Medium dark WRC		
Yellow pau amarillo		Medium light WRC		

Suggested raising and lowering

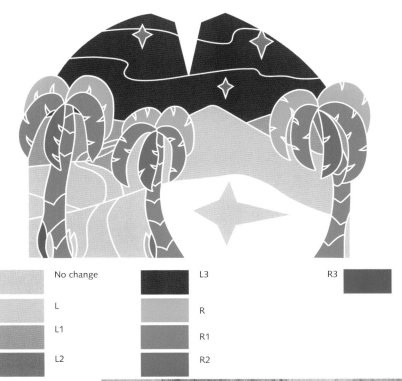

No change		L3		R3
L		R		
L1		R1		
L2		R2		

direction of wood grain
slope down

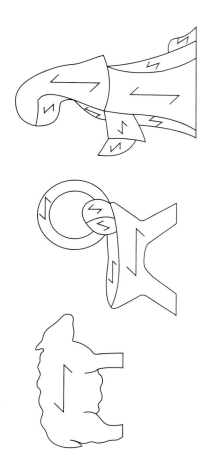

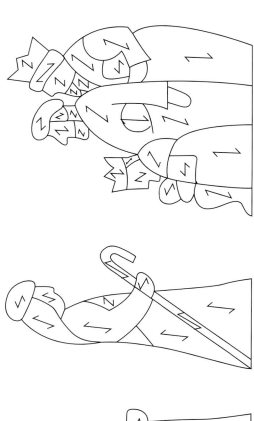

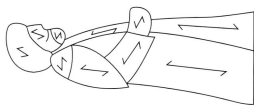

direction of
wood grain
slope down

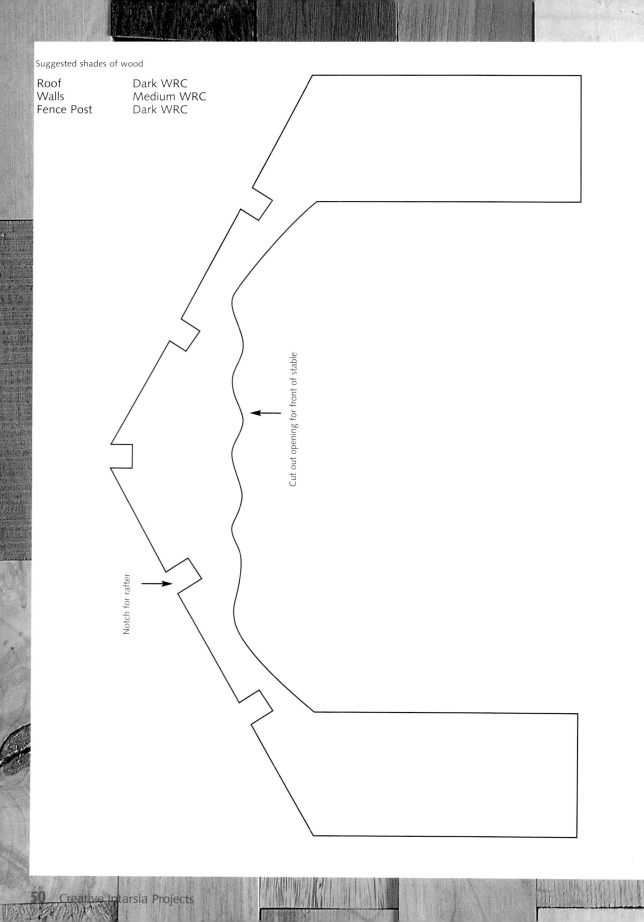

Suggested shades of wood

Roof   Dark WRC
Walls   Medium WRC
Fence Post   Dark WRC

Cut out opening for front of stable

Notch for rafter

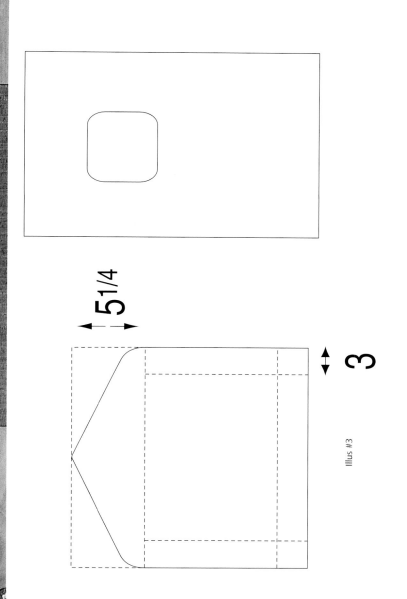

5 1/4

3

Illus #3

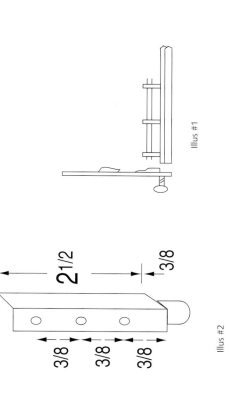

Illus #1

2 1/2

3/8

3/8 3/8 3/8

Illus #2

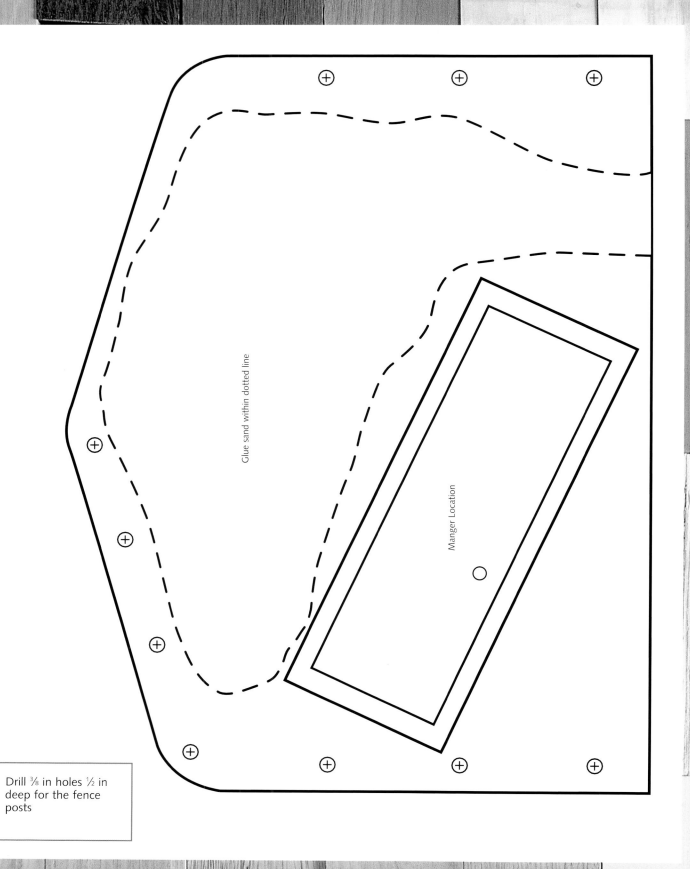

Glue sand within dotted line

Manger Location

Drill ⅜ in holes ½ in deep for the fence posts

Wizard and Dragon

Some man-made material is used in this project. It is made from strips of wood glued together under intense pressure. This method of producing wood products allows the industry to utilize smaller trees. The wood is used for support beams in buildings. The way you cut the beam changes the look of the wood. The piece I used for the dragon was cut across the ends of the strips. Cutting the grain at an angle creates interesting effects.

Above Use stamping to create scales on the wood surface *Center right* Place paint colors on a palette *Bottom* Close-up of flame paint on dragon's tail

Wizard and Dragon

The fantasy of wizards and dragons has been made popular with the movies of Harry Potter and the Lord of the Rings. In my version the wizard fights the dragon as part of the fire in its belly. This intarsia project utilizes a number of interesting effects such as staining and painting wood pieces as well as incorporating natural wood and stamping, and the use of stained glass for the fire. I used man-made wood (beam material at left) to create the interesting look to the belly of the dragon.

No. of pieces - 97
Finished size - 22 in x 22 in

Wood needed
Pine – 9 in x 20 in; 4 in x 18 in
Beam material – 12 in x 12 in
Dark western red cedar (WRC) – 6 in x 12 in
Light WRC – 4 in x 8 in
Medium WRC 6 in x 8 in
White aspen – 4 in x 4 in
Black walnut – 4 in x 4 in
Yellow pau amarillo – 2 in x 2 in

1 Enlarge (p10) the pattern on page 56 to the desired size.
2 Choose wood shades or types as pattern suggests, and transfer (p10) pattern to ¾ in thick wood.
3 Cut out the pieces carefully, making sure that the saw blade is square to the table (p11).
4 Assemble the pieces and check for fit. You may have to make some adjustments to the wizard to get it to fit into the dragon. The dragon's large arm attaches to the project with a dowel where it is marked on the pattern.
5 Raise and lower the pieces as the pattern suggests.
6 Reassemble the pieces and draw reference lines (p14). These lines will show how much to shape the pieces.
7 Shape the pieces to the reference lines to achieve a smooth transition from one level to the next.
8 Sand the pieces smooth with sandpaper or with a flap sander. There is no need to go over 220 grit.
9 Use a leather stamp to create the scales or use the end of a ⅜ in or ⁵⁄₁₆ in bolt to give a similar effect (p10). Dampening the wood makes stamping easier.
10 Burn in details of the dragon's eye with a wood-burning tool.
11 Paint the flames coming from the dragon's mouth, by the eye, and at the end of the tail. Place a strip each of red and yellow oil base interior paint on a palette or board. Do not mix them together but swirl the 2 colors into each other. Swirl strokes of color together to create the flame appearance.

12 Stain the body of the dragon green with oil base interior paint thinned with 20 percent paint thinner. Brush it on, leave for a few seconds, and wipe it off to the desired color, allowing the wood grain to show through. If the color is too light repeat the step. If it is too dark, allow to dry and then sand lightly.

13 Texture the wizard's beard with a wire brush to make it look like hair (p 10).

14 Use the wood burning tool and add details to the wizard's eyes, hat, and diamond on the sword handle (p9). You can also use a drafting ink pen.

15 The lines on the dragon nose and wizard face are cut with a scroll saw.

16 Paint the ball on the wizard's shaft dark green and the sword silver.

17 Finish all natural and stained wood pieces with a clear finish of your choice.

18 Choose a piece of stained glass that looks like fire from a stained glass shop and have the circle cut for you at the shop.

19 Assemble the project on the backing material (I used ¼ in Baltic birch plywood 24 in x 24 in which is strong and offers good support for the pieces). Use the set back method (p15) to attach backing. The back is cut out to accommodate the stained glass. The glass is cut slightly larger than the hole in order to glue it around the edges to the hole. I used Weldbond glue but epoxy or crazy glue suitable to glue wood to glass will also work.

20 Glue the project onto the backing material. Clamp.

21 Attach a hanger to the back to hang the project on the wall. For a very interesting effect mount a small light behind the project to shine through the stained glass.

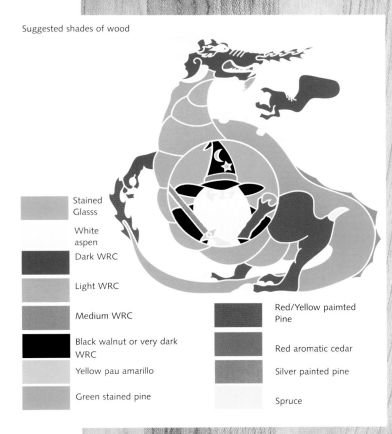

Suggested shades of wood

Stained Glasss	
White aspen	
Dark WRC	
Light WRC	
Medium WRC	Red/Yellow paimted Pine
Black walnut or very dark WRC	Red aromatic cedar
Yellow pau amarillo	Silver painted pine
Green stained pine	Spruce

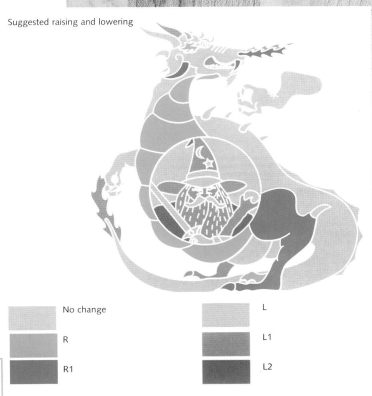

Suggested raising and lowering

No change	L
R	L1
R1	L2

Top Stained glass set into project resembles fire *Above* Back view of stained glass glued over the hole in the backing

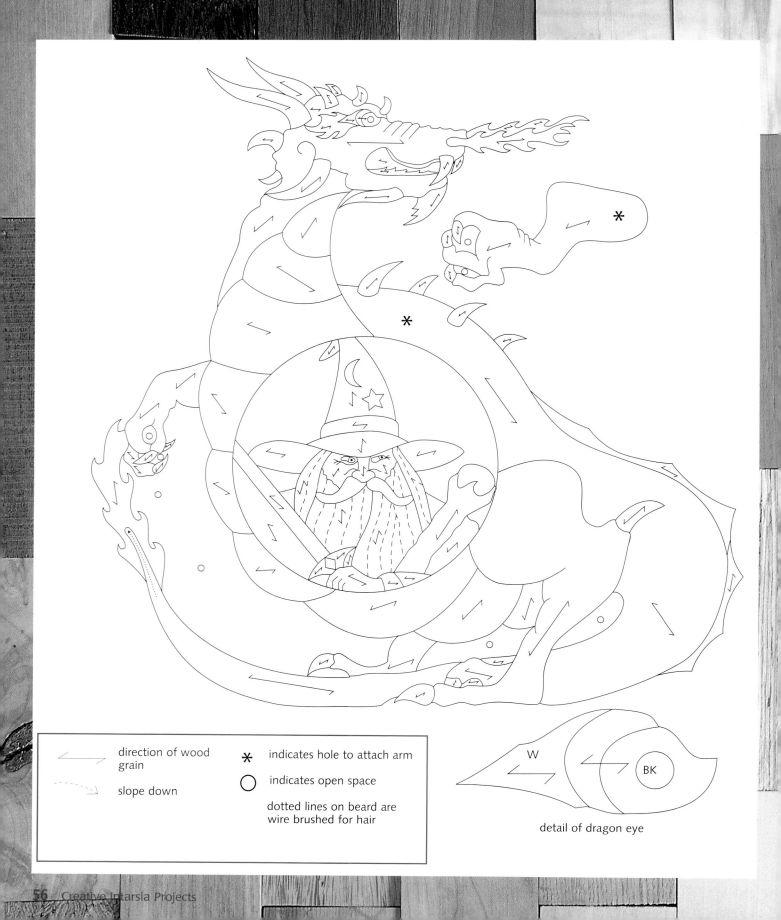

direction of wood grain

slope down

* indicates hole to attach arm

○ indicates open space

dotted lines on beard are wire brushed for hair

detail of dragon eye

W   BK

German Shepherd

German Shepherd

This popular dog breed is a favorite of many people. The project is quite easy to make and becomes a nice show piece to hang on any wall. I have included a few special effects techniques to add interest to the piece. The dog's expression is important and you may want to experiment with the eyes to produce the look you want.

No. of pieces - 35
Finished size - 8 in x 12 in

Wood needed
Dark western red cedar (WRC) – 6 in x 16 in
Medium (WRC) – 6 in x 6 in
Medium dark (WRC) – 6 in x 6 in
Light (WRC) – 6 in x 8 in
White aspen – 1 in x 2 in
Red aromatic cedar – 2 in x 3 in
Black walnut – 1 in x 2 in

1 Enlarge (p10) the pattern on page 60 to the desired size.

2 Choose wood shades or types as pattern suggests, and transfer (p10) pattern to ¾ in thick wood.

3 Cut out the pieces carefully, making sure that saw blade is square to the table (p11).

4 Assemble the pieces and check for fit.

5 Raise and lower the pieces as the pattern suggests (p13).

6 Reassemble the pieces and draw reference lines (p14). These lines will show how much to shape the pieces.

7 Begin to sand the pieces to shape them to the reference lines. Try to avoid flat edges.

8 Sand the pieces to 220 grit.

9 Use a wire brush in a flex shaft (p74) and brush the wood pieces to resemble the hair of the dog's coat. Dampen the wood to make the wire brushing more effective. I also use a fiber wheel to burnish the wood surface (p10, top right) to add realism to the look of the dog's coat. *Note* This step can also be accomplished with a hand wire brush.

10 The eyes of this project are important. I burned in the pupils for this project in several different ways from which you can experiment to find the expression you want. The dots on the muzzle are also burned in. The nostrils are black and the opening between the nostrils is scrolled out.

11 Reassemble the pieces onto the backing material, trace around them, and cut out the back. Glue the pieces onto the back with ordinary carpenter's glue.
12 Apply the finish of your choice. Allow to dry. Attach a hanger on the back of the project.

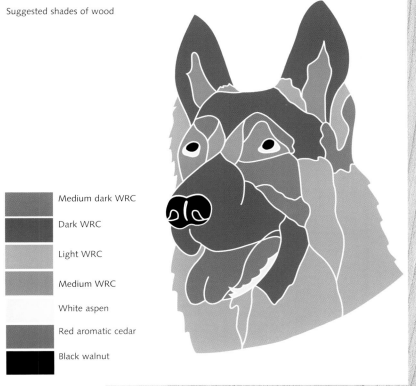

Suggested shades of wood

	Medium dark WRC
	Dark WRC
	Light WRC
	Medium WRC
	White aspen
	Red aromatic cedar
	Black walnut

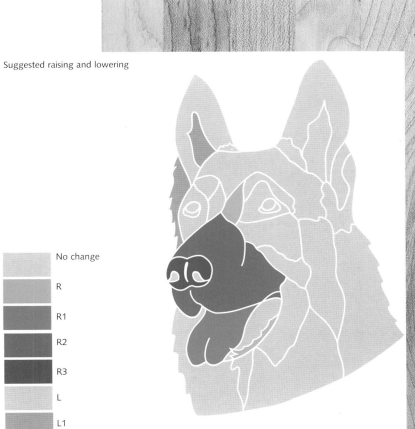

Suggested raising and lowering

	No change
	R
	R1
	R2
	R3
	L
	L1

   direction of wood
grain

slope down

Fish Through a Porthole

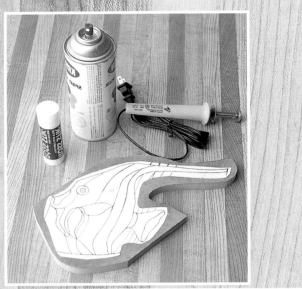

Fish Through a Porthole

If submarines had portholes is this a view you would see? This underwater scene incorporates many intarsia techniques. The wood used is MDF and pine – both easy to find. MDF (Medium Density Fiber) is a man-made material that is inexpensive and comes in a variety of thicknesses so that raising and lowering is already done, but the material does require painting. The fish and plants are nondirectional intarsia so wood grain is not important. Brass and stained glass are also used in this project.

No. of pieces - 112
Finished size - 17 ½ in diameter

Wood needed
MDF
¼ in – 3 in x 4 in
⅜ in – 6 in x 4 in; 2 in x 7 in
½ in – 5 in x 3 in; 3 in x 9 in
¾ in 9 in x 9 in; 3 in x 15 in
1 in   5 in x 5 in
Pine
1 in – 8 in x 48 in
Brass screws – 4
Brass (22 or 24 gauge) – 3 in x 6 in

1 Enlarge (p10) the pattern on page 64 to the desired size.
2 Choose wood thickness as pattern suggests and transfer (p10) the pattern to the wood. For nondirectional intarsia I glue the pattern to the wood , as shown left above.
3 Cut out the pieces carefully, making sure that the saw blade is square to the table (p11).
4 Use paint thinner to remove the paper pattern pieces after cutting out the pattern. Allow the thinner to soak into the paper and loosen the glue. A hot air gun also works.
5 Assemble the cut out pieces and check for fit. This project is easy to fit because the fish and plants are cut as one, as shown at left.

6 If you cannot find MDF boards in the varied thicknesses required for the project you can raise or lower at this time.

Read from top to bottom and left to right **1** Glue pattern to the MDF wood **2** The fish and plants are cut out as one piece from MDF so no fitting is required **3** Brass screws and brass plates give a realistic effect R*ight* **4** Choose stained glass that looks like sea water

7 Reassemble the pieces and mark reference lines (p14). These lines will show how much to shape the pieces.

8 Round the fish to give them a realistic look. Sanding MDF creates a lot of dust so be sure to wear a dust mask.

9 Sand the pieces by hand or with a flap sander. No need to go over 220 grit.

10 Drill holes in the frame for the brass screws. The ones I used have ¾ in heads. If you can't find brass screws use ¾ in dowel, cut a slot in it, and paint dowels gold.

11 Cut the brass with a #3 metal cutting blade or a #3 regular tooth blade.

12 Assemble the project and trace around the outside. Measure the inside diameter of the porthole. Cut this porthole ¼ in larger all around than the actual porthole which will leave a rabett in which to set the stained glass. Leave this backing board square so that it can be cut out later.

13 Finish the pieces at this time. Paint the fish and grass as indicated in the photo. Paint fish eyes, mouth and any lines. The frame looks nice with a walnut stain. MDF should be primed before it is painted. Allow to dry.

14 Choose a piece of stained glass to resemble seawater – dark blue with streaks of green and white.

15 Assemble the frame pieces and glue them to the backing on the lines drawn in step 12. Clamp where necessary.

16 Trim the square backing board round. Glue the stained glass in place. Allow to dry.

17 Assemble the fish and plants on the stained glass and glue in place using a white glue used for glass, wood, leather.

18 Attach a hanger on the back to hang the project on the wall.

Below Back of project shows how glass is attached, hanger at top

Suggested shades of wood

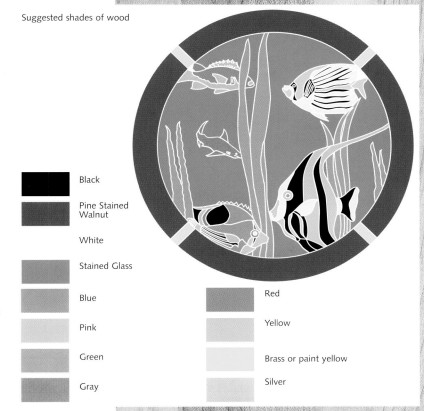

Black	
Pine Stained Walnut	
White	
Stained Glass	
Blue	Red
Pink	Yellow
Green	Brass or paint yellow
Gray	Silver

Suggested raising and lowering

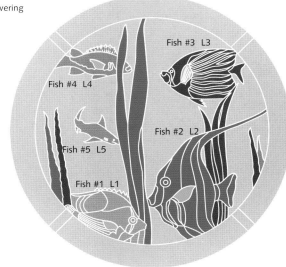

Fish #3 L3
Fish #4 L4
Fish #5 L5
Fish #2 L2
Fish #1 L1

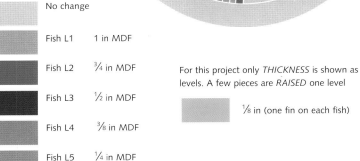

No change		
Fish L1	1 in MDF	
Fish L2	¾ in MDF	
Fish L3	½ in MDF	
Fish L4	⅜ in MDF	
Fish L5	¼ in MDF	

For this project only *THICKNESS* is shown as levels. A few pieces are *RAISED* one level

⅛ in (one fin on each fish)

direction of wood grain

position of brass screws

Above Parrot's eye and neck speckles are burned on *Center* Brush on paint and allow to sit for a few seconds *Bottom* Wipe off paint to achieve the desired shade

Parrot

This fun project creates a parrot that looks ready to fly away. The bright colors add realism and are very appealing. Since my project utilizes painting techniques and I like to see the wood grain through the stain, I am careful to cut each piece with the wood going in the right direction. However, some parts of this parrot can be cut as nondirectional intarsia. The parrot could also be made using natural woods choosing bloodwood for red, poplar for green, and blue cast spruce for blue. For a more traditional intarsia look use various shades of western red cedar.

No. of pieces - 58
Finished size - 14 in x 16 in

Wood needed
Dark western red cedar (WRC) – 6 in x 16 in
White – 4 in x 4 in
Black walnut – 4 in x 4 in
Pine (for the stained parts) – 6 in x 30 in
Yellow cedar (for the beak) – 3 in x 3 in

1 Enlarge (p10) pattern on page 68 to the desired size.
2 Choose wood shades or types as pattern suggests, and transfer (p10) to ¾ in thick wood.
3 Using the saw of your choice, square the blade to the table (p11) and cut out all pattern pieces on the line.
4 Assemble pattern pieces to check for fit. Pieces should fit together as closely as possible. A kerf saw width (¹⁄₁₆ in) between pieces is acceptable.
5 Raise and lower (p14) pieces as the pattern suggests.
6 Reassemble pieces and mark reference lines (p14) to aid shaping.
7 Using reference lines as a guide, shape to these lines to make a transition from one level to the next. Round the parrot's body as you shape to give it a realistic look. Try to avoid having flat edges showing.
8 When pieces are shaped to your liking, sand them with 220 grit or use a flap sander with 180 grit refill, which saves time.
9 Reassemble the project on the backing material and trace around the project.
10 Cut out the back but don't glue the pieces on at this time.
11 Use the wood burning tool to add parrot's eye, veins on leaves, marks on wings and tail, and neck speckles. If you don't have a wood burning tool use a drafting ink pen.
12 Choose parrot colors, as suggested in the color guide.

13 Prepare the stain by diluting oil base paint with thinner (half and half). Brush it on, as shown. Allow to sit for a few seconds and then wipe it off to give the desired effect.

14 When staining and wood burning are complete glue the pieces to the backing with white carpenter's glue.

15 Finish with a clear varnish of your choice.

16 Attach a hanger to the back for hanging on the wall.

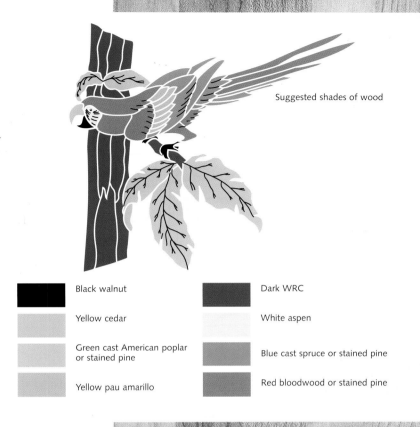

Suggested shades of wood

⬛ Black walnut		⬛ Dark WRC	
⬜ Yellow cedar		⬜ White aspen	
⬜ Green cast American poplar or stained pine		⬜ Blue cast spruce or stained pine	
⬜ Yellow pau amarillo		⬜ Red bloodwood or stained pine	

Suggested raising and lowering

⬜ No change		⬜ R1	
⬜ R		⬜ R2	

direction of wood grain

slope down

◯ indicates open space

Raccoon in a Tree

Raccoon in a Tree

This project shows how natural material (in this case a piece of tree) can be incorporated into a project to add interest and realism. The difficult part is to find the right piece of wood to give the effect you want. I found this piece after a long search. Everything in the project revolves around this forked branch that makes the project unique. The raccoon seems quite at home on this branch. The natural wood and the finished wood go together very well.

No. of pieces - 34
Finished size - 16 in x 12 in

Wood needed
Tree branch
White aspen – 6 in x 6 in
Dark western red cedar (WRC) –
6 in x 10 in
Medium WRC – 6 in x 10 in
Light WRC – 4 in x 4 in]
Black walnut – 2 in x 2 in
Backing material – 14 in x 18 in

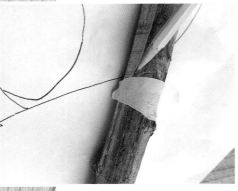

1 Find a tree branch about 16 in long with 1 to 1 ½ in diameter branches. Choose the branch from a dead tree so the wood will be dry.
2 Flatten the bottom of the fork on a belt sander.
3 Place the flattened fork on the raccoon pattern so that the fork fits in the pattern and mark the spots where the project and the tree fork will touch. Mark these areas with tape. Do not use pen or pencil because the mark will not come off without ruining the look of the tree fork.
4 Saw the edges where the project and the tree fork will meet.
5 Trace the trimmed fork onto the raccoon pattern.
6 Make a template of the raccoon pieces, leaving out the areas where the forked branch was traced.

7 Transfer the pattern to the wood with the template pieces.
8 Choose wood shades or types as the pattern suggests. Choose wood ¾ in thick.

Read from left to right Top **1** Find a forked branch from a dead tree **2** Flatten the forked wood on a belt sander **3** Use tape to mark where forked wood and project will touch **4** Saw the edges of the forked wood **5** Trace the forked wood onto the raccoon pattern **6** Make a template of the raccoon pieces **7** Drill holes for placement of leaf cluster

9 Cut out the pieces carefully, making sure that the saw blade is square to the table (p11).

10 Assemble the pieces and check the fit. The body of the raccoon must fit into the fork. The other pieces below the fork are fairly easy to fit.

11 Raise and lower the pieces as suggested by the pattern. Make the eyes from ⅜ in black walnut dowels.

12 Reassemble the pieces and draw reference lines. Begin shaping to these lines. Try to give the raccoon a rounded look. Do not round the pieces too much where they touch the tree fork.

13 Sand these pieces with a flap sander or by hand. Do not go over 220 grit.

14 Reassemble the pieces on the ¼ in thick 14 in x 18 in backing board, with the fork in place. Trace around the project. I used the set back method for the backing (p15).

15 Apply the finish of your choice. I did not put finish on the tree fork.

16 While the finish dries, make the leaf cluster. When the project is dry, attach leaves to the tree fork with dowels. Drill holes in the tree fork for the dowels. Use the photo as a placement guide.

17 Glue the project onto the backing board with ordinary white carpenter's glue.

18 Attach a hanger to the back to hang the project on the wall.

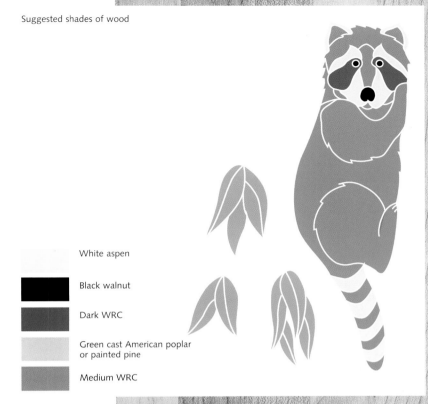

Suggested shades of wood

White aspen

Black walnut

Dark WRC

Green cast American poplar or painted pine

Medium WRC

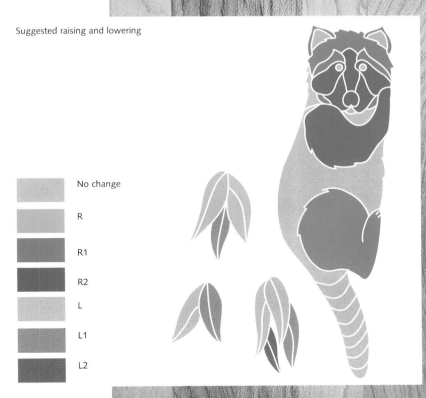

Suggested raising and lowering

No change

R

R1

R2

L

L1

L2

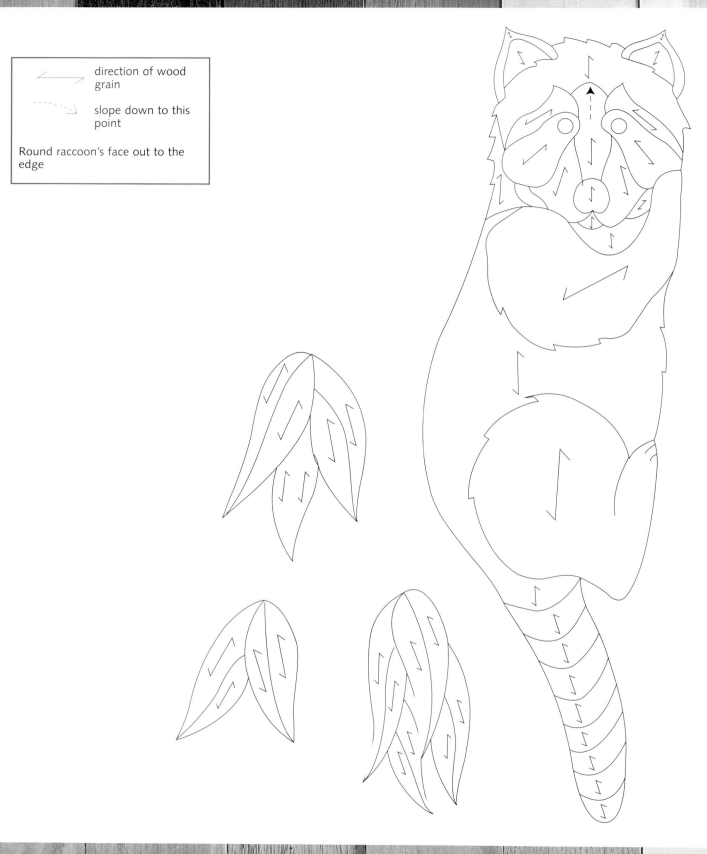

direction of wood grain

slope down to this point

Round raccoon's face out to the edge

Read top to bottom **1** Sanding out soft part of wood with a flap sander **2** Using a star twister to take out burned wood **3** Use a wire brush in a flex shaft to take out soft part of grain **4** Shows cone shape brush effect on wood

Eagle's Catch

The eagle is one of nature's most accomplished fishermen. The bird soars over the water, then swoops from incredible heights to nab its fishy prey. Such skill is amazing! For a number of years I stalked this majestic bird with my camera. I have hundreds of photographs but the three I like the best are the bird with head down eating the fish, the bird with wings extended swooping over the water about to strike the fish with its talons, and the bird with its catch as in this project, watching for another eagle who might steal the meal. My intarsia eagle sits on a piece of driftwood, holding the fish it has caught.

No. of pieces - 70
Finished size - 18 in x 20

Wood needed
Black walnut – 6 in x 20 in
White aspen – 6 in x 17 in
Yellow pau amarillo – 6 in x 6 in
Dark WRC – 6 in x 12 in
Medium WRC – 6 in x 6 in
Light WRC – 6 in x 6 in
Pine to texture and stain – 6 in x 24 in

Making Driftwood

"Where do I get driftwood?" you might ask. Not to worry. I have a tip given to me by a restoration artist in a museum and I am passing it on to you. Driftwood has a certain look. It has been affected over time by the elements. The wind creates grooves by eroding out the soft part of the grain. Time and the sun turn the wood a gray color, and cause cracks that fill with dirt, making black lines and shadows. To get this effect begin with a piece of pine with wide pronounced growth rings or any light colored softwood. Char the wood with a small torch (p40) to burn out the softer part of the grain. Do this on a metal surface such as a garbage can lid. Allow the burned wood to sit for 30 minutes before working further. At this time the wood is easier to groove with the flap sander, star twister, or sandblaster. You can also groove out the soft part of the grain with a wire brush placed in a flex shaft for this purpose. The flat brush is more aggressive while the cone shaped brush gives a different effect. Leave some dark areas, as shown at left for greater realisim. Repeat the charring and wire brushing a couple of times for deeper grooves and more resemblance to driftwood.

To achieve the gray weathered look make a stain with gray latex (water base) paint diluted with water (half and half). Wipe the stain on. Add more coats to make it darker or sand lightly for a lighter color. If you like the realism of driftwood with stones imbedded in the cracks, hammer in the stones of your choice and glue the stones in the indentations. Do not sand these areas.

1 Enlarge (p10) the pattern on page 76 to the size desired.

2 Transfer (p10) the pattern to ¾ in thick wood. Choose shade and color of wood pieces and grain direction as suggested on the pattern.

3 Cut out the project carefully, making sure the saw blade is square to the table (p11).

4 Assemble the pieces and check for fit. Match the pieces and the pattern with numbers which will help in the assembly in case pieces fall or get mixed up.

5 Raise and lower (p14) the pieces as the pattern suggests.

6 Reassemble the pieces and draw reference lines (p14), which will help to shape the pieces. Shape each piece down to these lines, and all the pieces except those for the driftwood log.

7 Sand by hand or with a flap sander. I don't sand past 220 grit.

8 Next, texture the wood for the driftwood piece, (p74).

9 Assemble the pieces on the backing material and trace around the project. Cut out the back. Use the set back method for this backing (p15).

10 Finish the pieces before gluing the project. I use an oil base varathane or urathane finish on most of these pieces, and I use clear latex finish on the white pieces and the driftwood because latex does not change the color of the wood. Allow to dry.

11 Glue pieces onto the backing material with ordinary white carpenter's glue. If the backing material is flat clamping won't be required.

12 Attach a hanger to the back to hang the project on the wall.

Above Dark areas in the wood grain give a weathered look *Below* Wipe on gray stain to give a driftwood look

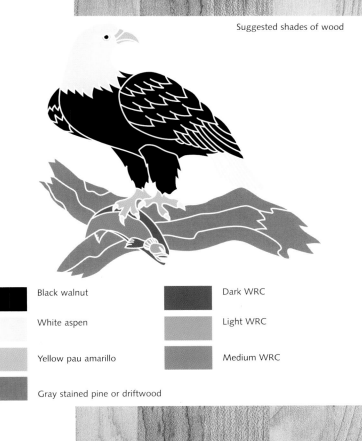

Suggested shades of wood

■ Black walnut			■ Dark WRC
White aspen			Light WRC
Yellow pau amarillo			Medium WRC
Gray stained pine or driftwood			

Suggested raising and lowering

No change			L
R			L1
R1			L2

direction of wood grain

slope down

○ indicates open space

Prairie Lilies

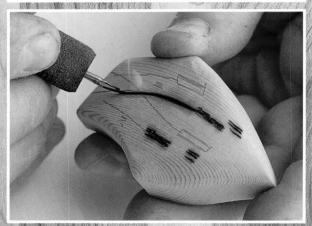

Read top to bottom **1** Shaping the leaves for the lily **2** Contouring the petals **3** Use a wood burning tool to burn spots on lily **4** Finished lilies with stemens and petal spots

Prairie Lilies

Part of the vastness and wonder of the Prairies is this beautiful, exotic flower, growing wild. Its deep orange color and delicate petals give it the appearance of a smaller version of the cultivated tiger lily. These rare wild flowers are protected by law in Saskatchewan and it is illegal to dig them up and transplant them. I thought if I wanted some for the house I'd have to make them. These intarsia lilies are enhanced by special effects techniques to add interest to the wood bouquet.

No. of pieces - 23
Finished size - 12 in x 9 in

Wood needed
Light western red cedar (WRC) – 6 in x 12 in
Green American poplar or medium WRC – 2 in x 3 in
Dark WRC– 2 in x 4 in

1 Enlarge (p10) a pattern on page 79 to the desired size.
2 Transfer (p10) the pattern to ¾ in thick wood. Choose the shade and color of wood and the grain direction for flowers and leaves.
3 Cut out the pieces carefully, making sure the saw blade is square to the table (p11).
4 Assemble the pieces and check for fit.
5 Raise and lower (p14) the pieces as the pattern suggests.
6 Reassemble the pieces and draw reference lines (p14) to guide the shaping of the pieces. Shaping in this project is important. The flowers should resemble the prairie lily. Shape the leaves carefully. Contour the petals and leaves on a flap sander to give a realistic look.
7 Sand all the pieces to 220 grit.
8 Burn in the stamens and petal spots with a wood burning tool. Reassemble the pieces on the backing material, trace around the pieces, and cut out the back. Glue the project with ordinary white carpenter's glue. If you keep the backing material flat you probably won't need to clamp.
9 Apply the finish of your choice.
10 Attach a hanger to the back to hang the project on the wall.

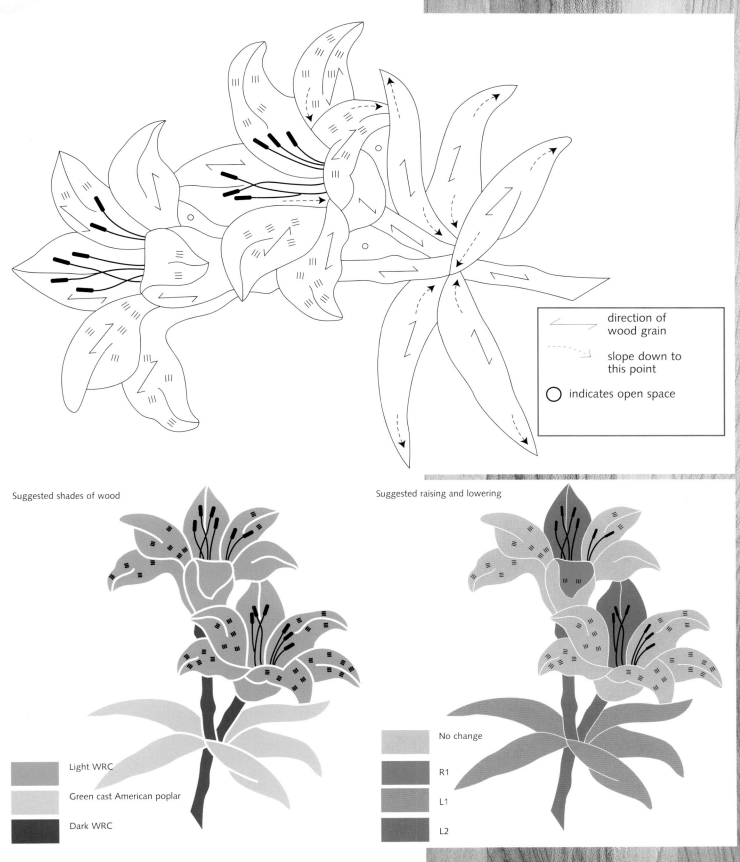

direction of
wood grain

slope down to
this point

○ indicates open space

Suggested shades of wood

Light WRC

Green cast American poplar

Dark WRC

Suggested raising and lowering

No change

R1

L1

L2

Mirror Art

Mirror Art

Almost any intarsia project can be turned into a mirror or framed piece to make it a functional work of art to decorate hallways or room settings. My regular intarsia project of a deer head was easily made into an oval mirror, with added cut outs for interest. The project pictured is for an oval mirror but you could make a round mirror with a duck (p25). A round mirror is easier for a first attempt. However, the oval mirror is not too difficult and depending on your woodworking skills you may want to make it first.

No. of pieces - 31
Finished size - 26 in x 16 in supposed to be round

Wood needed
Dark WRC – 6 in x 14 in
Black walnut – 2 in x 2 in
White aspen – 4 in x 6 in
Medium WRC – 4 in x 6 in
Medium dark WRC – 8 in x 36 in
Mirror glass -   26 in x 16 in

1 Transfer (p10) pattern to ¾ in thick wood.
2 Cut out the project carefully, making sure that the blade is square to the table (p11).
3 Assemble the pieces and check for fit.
4 Raise and lower (p14) the pieces as the pattern suggests.
5 Reassemble the pieces and draw reference lines (p14), which will help to shape the pieces.
6 Shape down to these lines to make a smooth transition from one level to the other.
7 Sand the pieces by hand or with a flap sander. I don't sand past 220 grit. Finish all the pieces with the finish of your choice.
8 To make sure no finish is on the bottom of the pieces, clean the bottoms on the belt sander.
9 Make the backing board (in this project it is a mirror). Make a template back (from inexpensive material or stiff cardboard). It should be ³⁄₁₆ in smaller than project. Take template to a glass shop and have mirror glass cut to size with small indentation in middle of top of mirror to attach hanger.
10 Assemble the project onto the mirror. It will be glued to the reflective side of the mirror. I used Weldbond and the glued pieces have remained firmly in place. Put glue on the bottom of the pieces and set them in place. Glue the frame pieces first. Use a minimum of glue on the glass because if it squeezes out it will be visible on the glass. Allow to dry overnight.

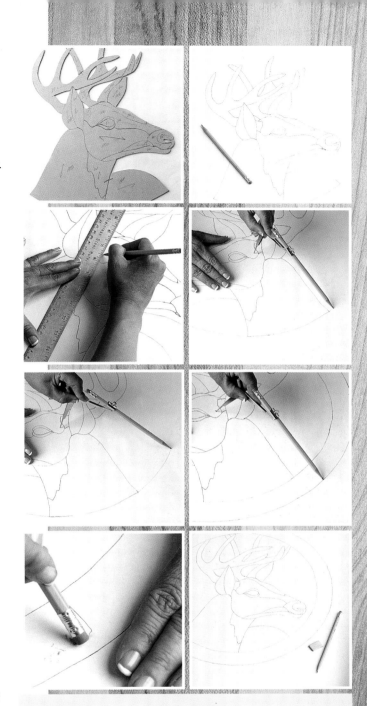

Making the Pattern for Round Mirror
Read left to right, **1** Lay the template for a mirror design onto white paper **2** Trace around it **3** Find the center of the project **4** Draw a circle for inside frame **5** Continue all around project **6** Again, from the center draw another circle for the outside frame **7** Erase the lines within the framed circle. **8** Now the pattern is ready for use. This basic technique can be used to make a frame for any intarsia piece and any mirror shape. Proceed as for any intarsia project. See instructions at left.

direction
of wood
grain

○ indicates open
space

saw tooth hanger

mirror

Suggested shades of wood

 Black walnut o

White aspen

 Dark WRC

Light WRC

Medium dark WRC

Suggested raising and lowering

No change

R

R1

L

L1

L2

Ducks in the Reeds

Ducks in the Reeds

This project utilizes found material and because of this offers the most opportunity to be creative. Choose from three different duck patterns (a mallard, a wood duck, and a diving duck) and place them according to your own vision. This project incorporates a number of different techniques and materials and resembles freestanding sculpture. It uses natural material, stained glass, painted surfaces, and unpainted wood.

No. of pieces	Finished size
Wood duck - 50	12 in x 10 in
Mallard - 36	12 in x 121 in
Diving duck - 16	5 ½ in x 5 ½ in

Wood needed

White aspen – 4 in x 6 in
Yellow pau amarillo – 2 in x 2 in
Black walnut – 1 in x 1 in
Dark western red cedar (WRC) – 6 in x 8 in
Medium dark WRC – 6 in x 8 in
Medium WRC – 6 in x 8 in
Medium light WRC – 6 in x 6 in
Light WRC – 6 in 8 in
Pine painted green – 6 in x 6 in
Pine painted blue – 2 in x 2 in
Baltic birch ⅛ in plywood – 1 sq ft for each duck and scraps for diving duck
Pine to paint – 2 in x 4 in; for reeds ¾ in square, 18 in long
Dowel – ⅛ in x 72 in long
Dowel – ¼ in x 1 in for duck eyes
Old wood - 4 pieces
Stained glass – 1 piece
MDF or pine for base – 9 in x 15 in x 1 in thick
Material for base frame – 9 in x 15 in x ¾ in thick.

This project is done in 2 steps: Ducks as regular intarsia projects and base with some different woodworking aspects.

1 Enlarge (p10) the pattern on pages 88, 89, 90 to size desired.
2 Choose wood shapes and types as pattern suggests and transfer (p10) pattern to the wood.
3 Using the saw of your choice, square the blade to the table (p11) and cut out the pattern pieces.
4 Assemble the pieces and check for fit.
5 Raise and lower (p14) pieces as the pattern suggests.
6 Reassemble the pieces and draw reference lines (p14) to guide in shaping the pieces from one level to the next. Shape down to these lines to form a smooth transition. Shape the ducks by sanding away everything that doesn't look like a duck.
7 Sand the pieces smooth to 220 grit.
8 Paint the pieces at this time. Allow to dry. An alternative to

Read from top to bottom, **1** Tree piece where wood duck will be attached **2** Tree branch is glued to stained glass **3** Countersink screws into bottom of base **4** Cutting reeds with scroll saw **5** Place strips in hot water for 10 minutes **6** Cut strips are fanned out to resemble reeds

paint is to use green cast poplar or vera wood for the green and bloodwood or padauk for the red in the construction of the ducks.

9 Assemble the project on some backing material (⅛ in Baltic birch plywood). Cut out the backing board.

10 Glue pieces onto the backing board with white carpenter's glue.

11 Drill a ⅜ in hole, ⅜ in deep in the back of the project. Where you drill the hole will depend on where you decide to place the duck.

12 Apply the finish of your choice. Allow to dry. Begin base.

13 Find a piece of dead tree 3 - 4 in diameter and 18 in long with knots or cracks, or some interesting feature. Cut off the bottom at an angle and sand flat. It should stand at about a 10 degree angle. The wood duck will be attached to this piece of tree. Next, find some larger knots that you can cut off the side of a branch. Sand these pieces flat. They will be glued onto the stained glass piece that you have chosen to resemble water. The reeds and cattails will be glued into these pieces.

14 Make the base at this time to fit the pieces you have found. I undercut the base about 15 degrees. This is painted black.

15 Cut a frame to go around the outside of the base top, ½ in wide and ¼ in deep, as shown. Glue on top of the base. The stained glass is placed inside this frame, as shown p84.

16 Make a template for the stained glass that will fit inside the frame. The long tree piece to which the duck will be attached must be attached to the base with two #8 – 1 ¾ in long wood screws. Holes will be drilled through the glass where you want tree to stand. Have holes drilled larger than screws (⅝ in).

17 Fit the glass into the frame and mark holes. Drill holes ⅛ in through the base as well as the countersink holes in the bottom (p84). Run screws from bottom so points come through surface and place tree over points. Push down and drill pilot holes where marks are. Glue glass into frame. Begin to tighten screws, careful not to break glass.

18 To mount the duck on the tree, hold duck to tree that has been attached to base. Position dowel in back of duck on the tree and make a mark for drilling a hole to hold the dowel. Drill a hole in the tree to hold the duck. Position it. When the glue dries it will stay in place.

19 Make the reeds from strips of pine or spruce ¾ in wide, ¼ in thick, and 10 in long. Cut lengthwise into strips with a scroll saw to about ⅜ in from the bottom. Strips will fan out. Place the strips in hot water for 10 minutes. Strips will bend and can be held in place with rubber bands. Shape the bottom of the reeds to a round shape (to place in hole in wood piece).

20 Make cattails from 2 pieces of black walnut ½ in x ½ in x 3 in long and ⅜ in x ⅜ in x 2 in long. Drill ⅛ in holes in each end for the stem and the white piece in the top. Shape the cattails on a belt sander or by hand or purchase a black walnut dowel. Drill ⁹⁄₆₄ in holes in wood pieces beside the reeds and push ⅛ in dowels into these holes.

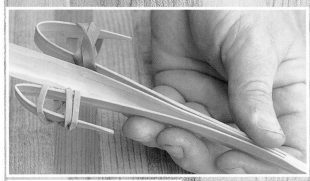

Read from top to bottom **1** Spread strips are held in place with rubber bands **2** Cattails made from black walnut pieces **3** Make holes in each end of cattail piece **4** Shape cattails on a belt sander

Suggested shades of wood   Duck #1

Black walnut or very dark WRC	Medium light WRC
White aspen	Dark WRC
Green cast American poplar	Light WRC
Yellow pau amarillo	Medium dark WRC
	Medium WRC

Suggested raising and lowering   Duck #1

No change	
R1	
L1	

21 Make holes for the reeds and cattails in the two pieces of wood you have chosen. For the reeds drill ³⁄₁₆ in holes side by side, move the drill back and forth to create an oblong hole. Shape the bottom end of the reeds to fit in this hole. Drill ⅛ in hole for the cattail stems. The placement of these pieces is your choice. Hold them in various places until you find what you like. Glue these pieces of wood to the glass. Apply the glue to the bottom and set in place. No need to clamp. Depending on the size of the base you made, there may be room for another piece and additional reeds and cattails.

22 Apply finish to the cattails but not the reeds. Do not put finish on the natural wood parts.

23 This freestanding piece is quite beautiful and well worth the effort of its construction.

Duck #2

Suggested shades of wood

Light WRC

Medium WRC

Medium dark WRC

Yellow pau amarillo

Dark WRC

Duck #2

Suggested raising and lowering

No change

R

R1

L

L1

Duck #3

Suggested shades of wood

Black walnut

White aspen

Green cast American poplar

Yellow pau amarillo

Dark WRC

Light WRC

Medium WRC

Blue painted pine

Duck #3

Suggested raising and lowering

No change

R

R1

R2

L1

Duck #1

direction of wood grain

Duck #2

direction of wood grain

slope down

Duck #3

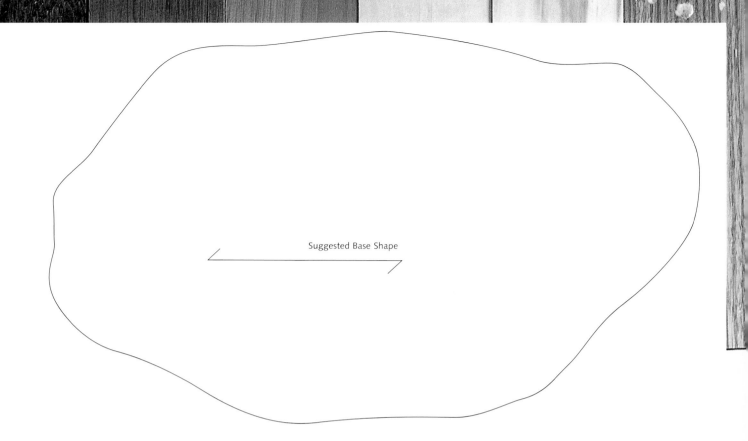

Suggested Base Shape

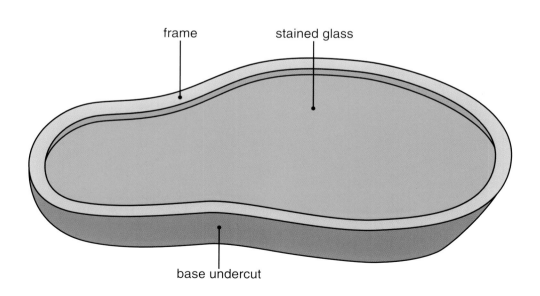

frame   stained glass

base undercut

Owl Bank

Cutting out the Bank Body

1 Glue together two 6 in wide x 14 in long x 1 ½ in thick for the bank body. Make sure the scroll saw is square to the table (p11). Use a precision ground (PG) style blade and cut carefully.

2 Once the back is cut out it tends to spring open. Tape it together with the pull-outs in place. 3 Trace the body onto a piece of ¼ plywood. Cut out the pull-outs. They will have to line up with the body pull-outs so cut carefully. The PG blades are too aggressive for plywood so choose a #3 double tooth or full reverse blade.

4 Drill or cut out the holes in the back to remove the coins.

Top **1** Cut out bank body *Center* **2** Use masking tape to hold pieces in place *Bottom* **3** cut out the back

Owl Bank

I include this bank for all my woodworking friends as a unique project that will test your skill and patience. This project is not for the faint of heart. The bank has three secret compartments, each with its own pull-out to disclose the coin slot. The bank is a challenge to make and requires perseverance to be sure all the parts line up in order for the bank to operate smoothly. However, the finished piece is worth the effort.

No. of pieces - 45
Finished size - 11 in x 12 ½ in

Wood needed
Pine for bank body – glue together two boards 6 in x 14 in x 1 ½ in thick
White aspen, holly, or basswood – 2 in x 4 in
Black walnut or very dark western red cedar (WRC) – 2 in x 4 in
Dark WRC or mahogany – 6 in x 8 in
Medium dark WRC – 6 in x 12 in
Medium dark WRC or cherry – 6 in x 8 in
Medium light WRC – 4 in x 6 in
Light WRC – 4 in x 6 in
Spruce or yellow cedar –
Backing material ¼ in Baltic birch plywood -11 in x 12 in; 11 in x 14 in

1 Enlarge (p10) the pattern on pages 94, 95 to the desired size.
2 Transfer (p10) the pattern to ¾ in thick wood, paying attention to shade, color, and grain pattern.
3 Cut out carefully, making sure saw blade is square to table (p11).
4 Assemble the pieces and check for fit.
5 Raise and lower (p14) the pieces as the pattern suggests.
6 Reassemble the pieces and mark reference lines (p14) to aid in shaping the pieces. Sand all the pieces to 220 grit.
7 Burn in the lines on the leaves with a wood burning tool.
8 Assemble the pieces on the backing board and trace around them. Cut out. *Note* The pieces on the pattern marked with a star have to slide back and forth. This is difficult to line up so you have to cut very carefully.
9 The intarsia project glued onto the backing becomes the front of the bank. With the body backboard temporarily attached, lay it on the front board and make sure the pull-outs line up. The front is bigger than the body so be sure it is even all around. The bottom of the tree of the body part must be even with the bottom of the tree with the intarsia part, in order for the piece to stand up. Mark the body and front again so they can be lined up for gluing. Glue the intarsia part. Allow to dry.
10 Round over the back edges of the backing board. (I make the backing board full size and chamfer or round out the edges (p15).

11 The 1 ½ in holes in each compartment have been cut out as marked on the pattern. Make the plugs from 1 ½ in dowels or use plastic inserts.

12 Glue on the body backing board, making sure pull-outs line up. Allow to dry. Glue on the intarsia front, making sure the pull-outs line up and slide in and out freely.

13 Sand the bottom smooth on the 6 in belt sander.

14 Finish the bank with three coats of the finish of your choice on the front and one coat on the back.

Top right **1** Back of bank *Center* **2** Putting coins in slot *Above* **3** Taking coins out of slot

Suggested shades of wood

Suggested raising and lowering

	Black walnut
	White aspen
	Medium light WRC
	Yellow cedar

	Dark WRC
	Light WRC
	Medium WRC
	Medium dark WRC

	No change
	R
	R1

	L
	L1

direction of wood grain

slope down

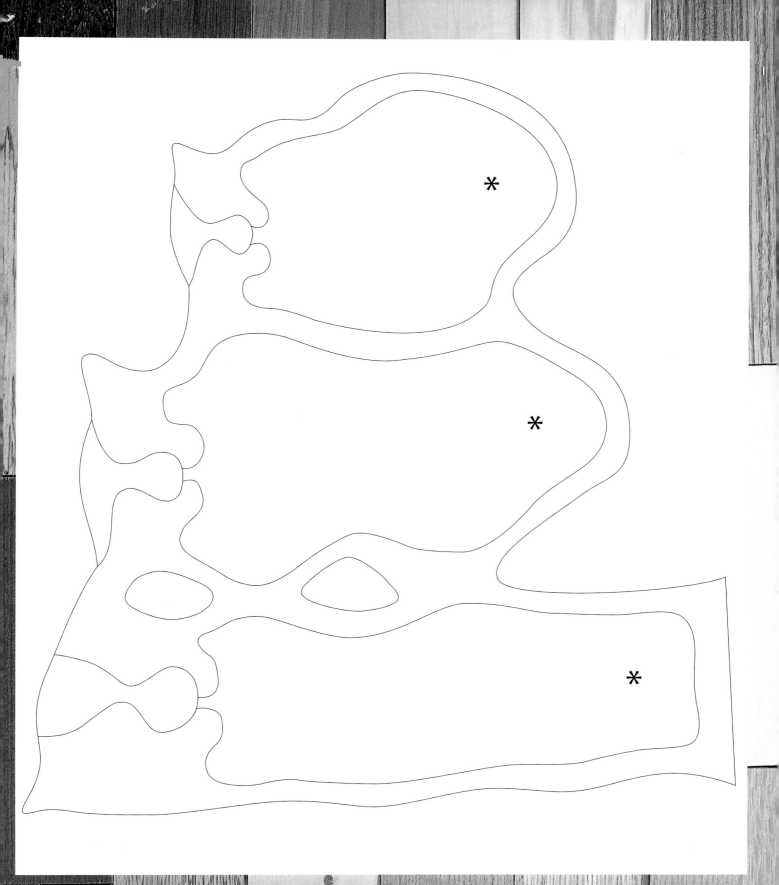

Index

acrylic, 25
adapter, 7
AFD, 18
aspenite, 23

backing, 14, 15
Baltic birch plywood, 11
band saw, 5, 6, 11, 14, 16, 17
base material, 14
beam material, 54
being creative, 24
belt sander, 7, 8
black edge plywood, 15
blade breaks, 17
blade lubricant, 5, 6
blueprint, 10
bolt ends, 10
burnishing, 4, 10, 58

carbon paper, 10, 11, 12
Carter stabalizer, 6
cattail making, 85
chamfered edge, 15, 40, 41
clock, 25
composite beam material, 23
cone shaped spiral sander, 8
cool blocks, 6
cutting small pieces, 16

dowel use, 28, 29
downdraft table, 18, 19
drafting ink pen, 67
Dremel tool, 8
driftwood, 4, 74
driftwood making, 74
drum sander, 8
drying wood, 23
duck#1 pattern, 88
duck#2 pattern, 88
duck#3 pattern, 89
Ducks in the reeds, 83
Ducks in the reeds base pattern, 90
dust, 18, 19
dust collecting system, 19
dust collectors, 18, 19
Eagle's catch, 73
Eagle's catch pattern, 76
electric motor, 7
emery boards, 7
enhanced 3-D, 4, 25
enlarging, 10
eye protection, 17

felt pen, 29
fiber wheel, 10
figurines, 45, 46
figurines pattern, 48
filters, 18
finishing, 16

fish eyes, 16
Fish through a porthole, 61
Fish through a porthole pattern, 64
fitting, 11, 12, 13
flap wheels, 8, 9
flex shaft, 7
Foredom carver, 7
forked tree branch, 70
found materials, 25, 84
freestanding, 3, 25, 35, 84
fuzzies, 5, 6, 7,

German shepherd, 57
German shepherd eyes, 58
German shepherd pattern, 60
glues, 11
gluing, 15
gluing pattern, 10, 62
goose#1 pattern, 30
goose#2 pattern, 32
goose#3 pattern, 33
grain textures, 20
grinders, 8

Haida art, 39
hardboard painted white, 15
hard rubber drum, 8
harmful fumes, 16

inside cuts, 6
interserere, 3

kerfs, 7

latex paint, 16, 74
leather apron, 17
leather gloves, 8
LeeValley jig, 13
lightbox, 12
loon, 25
loose clothing, 17

masks, 16, 18
MDF material, 14, 24, 62
metals, 25, 62
Merit flap sander, 8
Mirror art, 80
Mirror art pattern, 82
Mirror art pattern making, 81
mirror hanger, 82
mirrors, 25
Moonflight, 27

Nativity scene, 43
Nativity scene background pattern, 49
Nativity scene stand pattern, 52
natural material, 3
nondirectional intarsia, 24, 62, 66

Owl bank, 81
Owl bank pattern, 94, 95

Parrot, 65
Parrot pattern, 68

painted wood, 3, 24, 66, 84
paint thinner, 10
palm sander, 8
photocopy, 10
picture frames, 25
piggy banks, 24, 25
pizza box storage, 11
plastic inserts, 6, 16
plexiglass, 24
plicatic acid, 18
pneumatic sander, 7, 19
power carver, 7, 9
power rasps, 9
Prairie lilies, 77
Prairie lilies pattern, 79
push stick, 16
pyrography, 9

Raccoon in a tree, 69
Raccoon in a tree pattern 72
raising and lowering, 7, 14
raising and lowering guide, 13
Rearing horse, 34
Rearing horse pattern, 37
red cedar asthma, 18, 20
reed making, 84, 85
reference lines, 14, 39, 40
relief carving, 3
remaking a piece, 12
Rencrafts detail sander, 8
rounding blade, 6
rounding over bit, 15
router, 8, 15
runs, 16

safety, 16
safety apron, 17
sandpaper, 8, 9
Sandstrom sander, 7, 39
sandblaster, 4, 9, 10
sandblasting, 4, 9
sandblasting cabinet, 9
sanding cabinet, 19
sanding drums, 13
scrap plywood, 14
scroll saw, 5, 6, 7, 11, 14, 15, 25
scroll saw blades, 5
scrolling, 4
shaping, 7
simulating hair, 35
smooth edges, 5
spalted woods, 23
special effects projects, 24
special effects woods, 22
spindle sander, 13
squaring blade, 11
squirrel cage, 18
stained glass, 3
stained glass, 3, 25, 54, 55, 62, 63, 84
staining, 4, 24, 54, 55, 67, 75
stamping, 10, 54
star twister, 8

template, 11

tension gauge, 6
tension pitch, 6
texturing, 4, 40, 74
The Art of Intarsia, 15
Thunderbird, 38
Thunderbird pattern, 42
tighter turns, 6
torching, 36, 40
tracing pattern, 10
transfer tool, 11
twig stable, 43, 46, 47

unusual woods, 23

vacuums, 18
ventilation, 16, 17

water base finishes, 16
western red cedar darkening method, 20
western red cedar shades, 20
wire brushing, 10, 35
Wolfcraft flex shaft, 7
Wizard and dragon, 53
Wizard and dragon pattern, 56
wood burning, 4, 29, 66
wood burning tool, 4, 9, 28, 55, 78
wood colors, 20, 21, 22, 23
wood information, 2, 3
wood inlay, 3
wood stable, 43, 45, 47
wood stable pattern, 50, 51

zero clearance 6, 16

Direct your questions to
Garnet Hall email address
hall.intarsia@sk.sympatico.ca
Website - www.sawbird.com
Toll free number:
    1- 800 - 729 - 2473